THE HEART
OF THE MATTER

How PAPWORTH HOSPITAL transformed
modern heart and lung care

PETER PUGH

ICON

Published in the UK in 2015 by
Icon Books Ltd, Omnibus Business Centre,
39–41 North Road, London N7 9DP
email: info@iconbooks.com
www.iconbooks.com

Sold in the UK, Europe and Asia
by Faber & Faber Ltd, Bloomsbury House,
74–77 Great Russell Street, London WC1B 3DA or their agents

Distributed in the UK, Europe and Asia
by TBS Ltd, TBS Distribution Centre, Colchester Road
Frating Green, Colchester CO7 7DW

Distributed in Australia and New Zealand
by Allen & Unwin Pty Ltd, PO Box 8500,
83 Alexander Street, Crows Nest, NSW 2065

Distributed in South Africa
by Jonathan Ball, Office B4, The District,
41 Sir Lowry Road, Woodstock 7925

Distributed in India by Penguin Books India,
7th Floor, Infinity Tower – C, DLF Cyber City,
Gurgaon 122002, Haryana

Distributed in Canada by
Publishers Group Canada,
76 Stafford Street, Unit 300
Toronto, Ontario M6J 2S1

Distributed to the trade in the USA by
Consortium Book Sales and Distribution,
The Keg House, 34 Thirteenth Avenue NE,
Suite 101, Minneapolis, Minnesota 55413-1007

ISBN: 978-184831-942-4

Typeset in Dante by Marie Doherty
Printed and bound in the UK by Clays Ltd, St Ives plc

ABOUT THE AUTHOR

Peter Pugh was educated at Oundle and Cambridge, where he read History. He has written more than 50 official histories, including *The Magic of a Name*, a three-volume history of Rolls-Royce. He lives in Cambridge and Norfolk.

CONTENTS

Foreword   vii

Introduction   ix

Author's acknowledgements   xi

Monetary values   xiii

Chapter 1   Tuberculosis   1

Chapter 2   The Post-War World   37

Chapter 3   Heart Transplants   83

Chapter 4   Controversies   107

Chapter 5   Heart–Lung Transplants   141

Chapter 6   Mechanical Hearts   159

Chapter 7   Papworth's Range of Treatments   179

Chapter 8   Pulmonary Hypertension   221

Chapter 9   Putting Patients First   235

Chapter 10   The Move to Cambridge   255

Bibliography   279

Index   281

FOREWORD

by HRH *The Duchess of Gloucester*

We are fortunate to live in a country where a tradition has been built over many decades, if not centuries, of encouraging our finest brains to research into all matters medical. Consequently, Great Britain features prominently in many fields and the best researchers choose to come from all over the world to join our leading teams. Luckily, the general public enjoy contributing generously to projects where they can foresee the consequence of their support; nevertheless, it is essential that government funds also back these schemes.

Papworth Hospital has been an important element in this proud story. The 100 years that we are celebrating in this book demonstrate the battle against tuberculosis – a battle largely won, and the attention subsequently turned to organ transplants, pioneered at Papworth and now practised all over the world.

I hope that when the hospital moves to the Cambridge Biomedical Campus in the near future, it will not lose its many friends and supporters, who can be proud of the fact that a small place like Papworth should have such a big reputation internationally. I have no doubt that the high standards forever expected of its dedicated team of consultants, physicians, surgeons, nursing staff and support services and many more, will continue to provide life-changing, and in some cases lifelong, care for people who would otherwise struggle with their day-to-day lives, due to debilitating cardiothoracic conditions, and that the world will continue to notice Papworth Hospital's contribution to medical science for a long time to come.

Her Royal Highness the Duchess of Gloucester,
Patron of Papworth Hospital NHS Foundation Trust,
August 2015

INTRODUCTION

Papworth Hospital is a unique place.

This book documents how it has grown and adapted since its beginnings as an innovative TB sanatorium long before the majority of treatments we now take for granted were thought of.

It is now the largest heart and lung hospital in the UK and this evolution has taken place over the last 100 years on the same site.

But Papworth is not just a place, it's all about people, the patients whom the hospital treats and the staff who care deeply how that treatment is delivered. There is an intangible atmosphere of trust and sense of security which patients perceive, as well as a loyalty among all members of staff that is engendered. This combines to give Papworth a culture and ethos that sets it apart.

As we approach the 100-year anniversary and the move to our new hospital happens in the same year, it is that culture which we have to transfer as well as the technical, medical and surgical expertise. This will ensure Papworth continues to give the best of care to all our patients.

With the development of a world-class research and education institute alongside the hospital we will maintain the world renown and reputation which Papworth has deservedly earned.

Professor John Wallwork CBE
August 2015

AUTHOR'S ACKNOWLEDGEMENTS

The history of Papworth Hospital, *The Heart of the Matter*, was a particularly challenging, but fascinating, story to research and write and many people were helpful in allowing me to interview them and then, in some cases, checking that what I had written was accurate.

I would like to thank especially Stephen Bridge, the Chief Executive, and Professor John Wallwork, a long-serving consultant surgeon at Papworth Hospital and currently Chairman of the Board of Directors. They gave me the list of interviewees and read and corrected my draft manuscripts.

These were the interviewees, all of whom were most helpful:

Sir Terence English, John Dunning, Simon Fynn, Peter Schofield, Charles Haworth, John Shneerson, Bill Newsom, Julia Fleming, Stephen Large, Samer Nashef, Francis Wells, Ian Hardy, Alain Vuylsteke, Chris Flower, Keith McNeil, Susan Stewart, David Stone, Bob Verney, Michael Petch, Mrs Ellen Kemp, Celia Hyde, Natalie Doughty, Donna Ward and Hazel Farren.

Sir Terence English also provided a great deal of important archive material. (As it happens, Sir Terence and I were on a parent/teachers' committee at St John's College

Prep School at the time he carried out the first UK heart transplant.)

On the administrative side, many were very helpful, especially Barbara Gamble, Rebecca Proctor, Roger Hall, Daniel Saxton, Colin Lattimore, Hazel Crawford, Craig Mackenzie and Rachel Allen.

As always, when my books are published by Icon Books Ltd, the Editorial Director, Duncan Heath, masterminded the copy-editing, proof-reading and indexing. The cover design and organisation of the photographs were handled by Oliver Pugh of Simmons Pugh.

Peter Pugh, August 2015

MONETARY VALUES

Money and its value is always a problem when writing about a period that stretches over a number of years, particularly when parts of that period have included some years of very high inflation. Furthermore, establishing a yardstick for measuring the change in the value of money is not easy either. Do we take the external value of the £ or what it will buy in the average (whatever that may be) weekly shopping basket? Do we relate it to the average manual wage? As we know, while prices in general might rise, and have done so in Britain every year since the Second World War, the prices of certain products might fall. However, we are writing about a hospital, which, in some ways, is like a business, and money and its value crop up regularly. We therefore have to make some judgements. We can only generalise, and I think the best yardstick is probably the average working wage.

Taking this as the yardstick, here is a measure of the £ sterling relative to the £ in 2015.

Apart from wartime, prices were stable for 250 years, but prices began to rise in the run-up to the First World War.

1665–1900 multiply by 120
1900–1914 multiply by 110
1918–1939 multiply by 60
1945–1950 multiply by 35
1950–1960 multiply by 30
1960–1970 multiply by 25
1970–1974 multiply by 20
1975–1977 multiply by 15
1978–1980 multiply by 8
1980–1987 multiply by 5
1987–1991 multiply by 2.5
1991–1997 multiply by 2
1997–2010 multiply by 1.5

Since 2010, the rate of inflation, by the standards of most of the 20th century, has been very low, averaging, until very recently, less than the government's originally stated aim of 2.5 per cent (since reduced to 2 per cent). Some things such as telephone charges and many items made in the Far East, notably China, are going down in price while others, such as houses, moved up very sharply from 1997 to 2008 before falling back in the financial crisis. In 2011 on the back of sharply rising commodity and food prices, inflation accelerated again to reach 5 per cent per annum. However, as commodity prices fell back and much of the world suffered very low growth, the rate of inflation began to subside again in 2012 and 2013. Indeed, by 2015 many of the industrialised nations were starting to worry about deflation, which can be equally damaging as runaway inflation as consumers delay purchases and businesses delay investment.

Chapter 1

TUBERCULOSIS

The killer
Varrier-Jones
Papworth Colony
Achievements of a great man

The killer

Papworth Hospital was founded in 1918 by the social pioneer, Dr (later Sir) Pendrill Varrier-Jones, who named it the Cambridgeshire Tuberculosis Colony. The colony began in the village of Bourn near Cambridge in 1917 but, in 1918, when he had raised enough funding (£6,000 or about £360,000 in today's money) to buy Papworth Hall, Varrier-Jones moved the colony to the village of Papworth Everard. The purchase of the Hall included most of the land in the village and the colony rapidly expanded.

Varrier-Jones's aim was to rehabilitate tuberculosis, or TB, sufferers by providing treatment for them, consisting of surgery and fresh air, and also by offering employment and housing.

In his book, *On the Road: The Papworth Story*, published in 1977, Rowland Parker explained the history of TB very well. This is what he wrote, with some modifications and additions:

The presence of a tubercle bacillus had been suspected before 1882, and something of his nature known as early as 1865, when it was proved that Mike [Parker called TB 'Mike'] could be transmitted from one person to another, though that also had been suspected. It was Dr Robert Koch, a German scientist, who discovered and identified him. Hats off to Dr Koch, and all due credit to the craftsmen and technicians who made his microscope, without which Mike would not have been seen to be discovered, for he is a very little fellow. Robert Koch, with Friedrich Hoffler, formulated the postulates to describe the causes of cholera and tuberculosis.

A little devil, shaped rather like a minuscule bit of ver-micelli, he has no dimensions on his own. Take a box with a capacity of one cubic millimetre; fill it right up with TB, and you have a quarter of a million.

TB's object in life, like that of so many more of God's creations, was, so far as humans could judge, simply to be and to go on being. TB's favourite haunt was the lung of a human being, though it could happily reside in the bones, the throat, the intestines or the blood-stream, and did not mind hanging about in the air for a few hours before finding a home. One variety of TB lived in the milk and milk-producing organs of cattle, and another, much smaller in number, in the bodies of certain birds. They all liked lungs, because it was so easy to get there. One deep breath, and there they were.

Once there, TB lost no time in getting down to the job of reproduction, feeding on the tissue of the lung and so destroying it by forming little nodules which grew, ulcerated, then collapsed in the middle, leaving a crater from which the next generation of TB emerged to go and start another nodule not far away. Several square inches of lung soon became 'nothing but holes'. The effect was rather like that of rust on a car body, inadequately cared for. But whereas the busy or negligent car owner could see what was happening, the unfortunate host of those parasitic guests may not have been aware for several months, or even years, that they were there. Awareness began with sweating in the night, coughing and spitting; then more coughing and spitting; loss of weight and energy; then spitting of blood, denoting that the lung was suffering

4

serious damage. Then – if nothing was done – death. Babies died before the blood-spitting stage was reached.

Here is a more cheerful note. The human body did not take this parasitic invasion lying down. It fought back. If the lungs could be filled constantly with clean fresh air; if the amount of energy expended by the body was reduced to a minimum; if the fighting-back mechanism was reinforced by good wholesome food; and if those conditions were provided early enough, before the degree of infection was too great, the body would win. TB would give up the struggle.

The disease, aptly called 'consumption' (the names 'phthisis' and 'tuberculosis' are relatively recent) had been known for centuries; the symptoms clearly recognised before the nineteenth century. As diagnosis became more accurate and statistical information accumulated, TB was eventually seen to be what for a long time it had been suspected of being: Killer No. 1. In the year 1837, in an area comprising Cambridgeshire, Huntingdonshire and South Lincolnshire, 3,048 people died. Of these, 585 died of 'consumption' bracketed with 'decline'. That was more than double the number of deaths from any other single cause, and should almost certainly be increased by transfer from the totals registered as dying of 'pneumonia', 'disease' and 'causes not specified', the latter being next highest on the list, with 'old age' a good third. And that, be it noted, was in an area where fresh air was plentiful and malnutrition well below the average.

Fresh air in particular was early recognised as a contributory factor, if not to a cure, at least to a prolongation of life in consumptives. In the 1870s and 80s 'sanatoria' were established in localities where the air was considered to be wholly free from pollution – 'wholesome' was the word – and Switzerland headed the list, though almost any mountainous area served as well. This added a further element to the 'consumption syndrome', already highly charged with emotion. The rich were able to go abroad for expensive care and possible cure; the poor were obliged to stay in their crowded city slums and slowly die. Consumption became a 'fashionable' disease even in its real state. It was adopted by some wealthy people as an excuse for spending years in idleness, basking in sunshine and sympathy, and paying exorbitant fees for the privilege. The fatality of the disease afforded admirable scope for dramatists, novelists, librettists and writers of moral stories for the young, particularly as its incidence was very high in young females.

The cough of a Mimi or a Violetta would reach the heart no less surely than one of her purest notes. The blood-spotted handkerchief had more dramatic impact than a whole chapter of words. Meanwhile the wretched poor, and those less poor but just as wretched, continued to die in their thousands.

For it was one thing to diagnose; an altogether different thing to cure. The medical world did what it could. An injection of carbolic was tried in a few cases; the surgeon's knife was tried (actually it had been tried two centuries earlier!). It was generally realised that the disease need not be a killer, given early diagnosis and proper care. It was known that hundreds of thousands of cases, all potential spreaders of the disease, were at large. In 1887 Sir Robert Philip of Edinburgh inaugurated specific measures for control on the principle of careful supervision and a serious effort to improve the standard of living. The machinery of State and Local government took a long time to get wound up. In 1907 the Local Government Board urged voluntary notification of the disease, but it was not until 1911 that regulations were issued making notification of all cases of pulmonary TB compulsory. (The same regulations imposed fines for spitting in certain places, and gave rise to the 'joke' about the two old ladies at the concert where the band played the 'Refrain from Spitting'.)

Sanatoria were erected all over the country, some managed by private philanthropic agencies, others by local authorities, Counties or County Boroughs. The treatment once available only for the rich became the commonplace of the poor. County TB Officers were appointed. The State was in the battle against TB.

It undoubtedly slowed its march. But the casualties were still such as to render illusory whatever victory was claimed. Of those discharged from sanatoria, classified as having had the disease 'arrested', between one third and two thirds died within five years of leaving, most of them within two years. Nobody knew what it was costing the country in cash. (Dr H. Biggs in 1903 estimated that it was costing the USA £66,000,000. Sir A. Newsholme estimated that the eradication of TB would save Great Britain £10,000,000 [£1 billion in today's money].)

Varrier-Jones

As Rowland Parker wrote in 1977 in his book *On the Road*:

> That was good enough for Varrier-Jones. If it could be done, it would be done. He talked to all the right people. That was another of the assets of this man – he knew all the right people. If he did not already know them, he soon made it his business to get to know them. He already had the willing cooperation and backing of his chief, Professor Sir C. Allbutt, KCB, who was largely instrumental in forming, on Dec. 2nd 1916, the Cambs. Tuberculosis After-Care Association, the independent authority which was needed to put V-J's scheme on an official footing. Friendly Society members (there were only fifteen of them in the county) in need of TB after-care would get ten shillings a week to begin with, less as they got stronger. Non-members would be helped from subscriptions – there would not be more than five of them at any one time, it was thought. The aim of the After-Care committee was to raise a fund of £100 a year to begin with. It was not much – but it was something. That was in January 1917.
>
> Committee meetings take time. People have other equally important things to do; their own lives to live. There was a war on. Varrier-Jones could not wait for official progress. It would catch up with him in time, perhaps. Having started things moving in one sector, he went off on his own to get the money to start doing while the committees were still talking. Not that he was impatient with them. He was just downright damn-well-determined

to get something done. He begged, bullied and cajoled £603 [about £36,000 in today's money] out of the local worthies. (The contributions included £10 from P.C. Varrier-Jones, Esq. MD.) He begged a green-house, garden tools, a governess-cart, a harmonium; provided his own croquet-set and 'clinkers'; formed a committee; bought a house at Bourn and established the 'Cambridgeshire Tuberculosis Colony' in February 1916 (eleven months before he had official backing). The Colony consisted of six patients and a nurse! Never mind, it was a start. He was off the ground. Wrong idiom for that date – he was on the ground. By August of that year the personnel numbered nineteen; fourteen patients, three nurses, Matron and V-J. There were 48 'Governors'.

In June 1917 the After-Care committee caught up with him; it and the Colony joined forces. The latter was approved by the Local Government Board as an 'Institution for the Treatment of early cases of Pulmonary and Surgical Tuberculosis'. (I wonder what would have happened if they had disapproved!) The staff lived in the house, the patients in open-air shelters which they had made. A word about these 'shelters', since they were to become a sort of jocular legend, and are still in fact. They were really just wooden boxes about seven feet square, with a pyramidal roof, three sides being fitted with canvas screens which could be raised or lowered as required; so that the occupant was virtually indoors and out of doors at the same time; in all weathers – a waterproof sheet being provided to keep the worst of the rain and snow off his bed. Bath-room, lavatories, dining and recreation room were arranged. 'Continuous temperature records were registered' – I take that to refer to the temperature of the patients, not the air, which in that first January was perhaps best left unrecorded. The charge per patient was thirty shillings a week. The patients did all the work which had to be done to get the Colony ship-shape – cutting down trees, making paths, draining, cultivating the garden. They designed and planned everything, and 'showed the keenest interest in the work'. Listen to one of them, writing anonymously in the 'Papworth Annual' of 1942:

'It was the second year of the Great War. Some of my colleagues were soldiers of recent experience, and what experiences they recounted, and how they appreciated the luxury of beds and wooden huts! – F.S. and his home-made barometer – the Scot who very much resented the ice in his toilet water-bottle – the nightly sing-songs after lights-out at 8 p.m. The little house, the Sister, the Cook – and what a kind soul she was to all the lads – and last but not least Dr Varrier-Jones, his morning and evening rounds; how we looked forward to them – his readiness to answer questions, and not always medical questions at that – his astonishment at much of the truth we told him regarding the working-man's wage, and how it was spent! – F.S. was the first to be put on work, one hour in the morning and one hour in the afternoon – the first obvious piece of constructive work was to drain the pond – F.S. dug a trench in the course of a few days, and so well was his work carried out that without due warning the village of Bourn was well-nigh flooded out! The second patient for work wished to look after the chicken-farm – I doubt if any twenty hens were ever so well cared-for before or since. What a happy party we were, more like a family, each with a self-appointed duty for the patients confined to their beds.'

If any of my readers suppose that Varrier-Jones rested on his laurels and preened himself on having done a good job, then I have made a bad job of depicting his character so far. He was already planning the next move before the first move was anything like complete. I spoke earlier of the 'path of destiny'. It will be noticed that Bourn is only about five miles from Papworth. Fate did not arrange that. But Fate, surely, arranged that Papworth Hall should still be empty, and for sale, just when Varrier-Jones was looking for somewhere to go next. If Buckingham Palace had been empty, and for sale, and a bit nearer, he would doubtless have gone for that. (As a matter of fact he did, in a different sense, a bit later.) He was not a man; he was a dynamo; a dynamo with a head, a heart and a voice.

He used all three to good effect. The Rt. Hon. Sir Ernest Cassel came up with a cheque for £5,000 [£300,000 in today's money]; others, most of them 'Governors', added £1,338; the Institutional Committee of the Government granted £3,000; and an anonymous donor, with the purchase of the 23 acres of woodland in mind, raised the sum to just over £9,600. Which, by an odd coincidence, was the very sum the committee needed to purchase the

Hall (£6,000), lay on a water-supply, make the necessary structural alterations, buy furniture (of a slightly different pattern from that of Cheere or Hooley [see below] and leave a bit over for a working balance and incidentals. Who but a Varrier-Jones would have had the courage to leap at such an opportunity, bristling as it was with problems and difficulties? It was not that he did not see the problems. What he saw most clearly was the opportunity. The fences beyond the next would be jumped when he got there.

At this point, lest it be forgotten in the whirl of events to come, I must pay due tribute to those people – and they were many, too many to be named individually – who supported this dynamic man, not only with money, but with faith. He could not have achieved what he did without them. They perhaps would not have done what they did without him. The greatest asset of all those which Pendrill Varrier-Jones possessed was perhaps this – his ability to inspire in others the faith which he had in himself.

The Bourn colony was established not just by the doctor and nurses but by the patients. Varrier-Jones sought the opinions and the expectations of his patients, the foundations of a self-governing community were being laid.

So the Colony moved from Bourn to Papworth Hall. Let my anonymous informant tell it his way:

'Shall I ever forget that cold bright sunny morning in February, 1918, when we moved, seventeen patients and four staff? How excited we were to pack our luggage, beds and shelters; and the discussion as to how we were to travel! Laddie, the pony in the Jingle, took three patients. Others travelled by car. One youthful member, H.L., had the loan of Dr Varrier-Jones's bicycle, and so arrived earlier than the majority. (The beds and shelters went on farm-carts borrowed for the occasion.) How we admired the Hall, the lake and the gardens, and how busy we were, or thought we were, helping to erect our shelters for the night.'

Charles Madryll Cheere had built Papworth Hall to impress the county. Ernest Terah Hooley had bought and used the Hall to impress the country. For example, he hosted large, ebullient parties giving rise to the name 'Hoolies'. Pendrill Varrier-Jones was not out to 'impress' anybody. Yet in the space of less than twenty years the name of Papworth was to be known throughout the world.

The Colony was no sooner planted than it started to grow at an astonishing speed. Varrier-Jones's knack of knowing the right people, and skill at getting them on his side, brought him into contact with Sir Frederick Milner ('the Soldier's Friend') and through him the support of the Royal Family was secured. On Oct. 9th 1918 Her Majesty Queen Mary, accompanied by HRH The Princess Royal, paid what was to be the first of many royal visits to Papworth. 'What a gala day for everybody! And how it rained! And the mud! Did ever royal visitors give more pleasure and encouragement to the sick and to those struggling back to health?'

The Colony at that time consisted of 25 shelters, 60 beds in the Hall, eight cottages and five 'industries'; these latter being carpentry and cabinet shops, boot-repair shop, poultry-farm, fruit-farm and piggery. Not bad for eight months' effort!

In 1921 there were 200 men, mostly ex-soldiers, under treatment; 140, along with 25 convalescents living in the settlement, were undergoing a course of training. A new Village Store had been opened; St John's Hospital opened; St Peter's House became a Nurses' Home; a new drainage-system was completed, and 28 cottages were erected by the County Council. There was no marking time on any sector of the front. The 'Sims Woodhead' Research Building opened in 1923, and 'Homeleigh' (once Home Farm) developed as a hostel for women. A grant from the Government enabled the construction of 25 new cottages which were formally opened on July 23rd as 'York Cottages' by Their Royal Highnesses the Duke and Duchess of York. Never before had so many people visited Papworth, for it was Flower Show Day.

Encouraged by success, undeterred by failure, Papworth had to go on. There were more cottages, new hostels, new workshops, recreation-rooms, etc. In 1930 there were 200 men and 80 women patients; 294 on average were in daily employment; the Industries had an annual turnover of £68,000. Royal visits became a commonplace, but none the less appreciated for that: Duke and Duchess of York in 1927, 1929 and 1932; The Duke of

Windsor (then Prince of Wales) in 1928; HM Queen Mary in 1929, 1933, 1939 and again in 1945; on July 26th, 1934, HRH The Duke of Gloucester opened the Bernhard Baron Memorial Hospital and laid the foundation-stone of the new Surgical Unit. 'What a good speech he made. Another sunny happy day.'

On 28 October 1932 *The Times* reported:

Grant From Bernhard Baron Trust
The growing needs in the fight against tuberculosis of the Papworth Village Settlement have been further met by a grant from the Bernhard Baron Trustees for the building of a hospital and today the foundation stone was laid by Lady Baron.

The new hospital which will be erected so far as possible by skilled workers in the colony and which has been designed by Mr McMahon, manager of the building department and Mr Copse, both of whom have been patients at the Settlement, will accommodate about 84 patients and will also contain an out-patients department for the use of the whole village.

And on 4 July 1932, *The Times* reported:

The Queen signified her intent to being present at [the play] *The French Picture* in aid of Papworth Village Settlement.

Followed by, on 9 July 1932:

ROYAL VISIT TO CAMBRIDGE
New Wing Opened at Addenbrooke's
The Duke and Duchess of York visited Cambridge and the Papworth Village Settlement today. The occasion was the opening of a new women's hospital at Papworth and an important addition at Addenbrooke's.

Arriving at Papworth the royal visitors were met by Sir Humphrey Rolleston and the Medical Director, Sir Pendrill Varrier-Jones. They proceeded to the new building where the Duchess unveiled a tablet and declared the hospital open. The design, construction and furnishing have been done by Papworth Industries and the designers who are ex-patients at the colony, have embodied in the hospital novel features whose value was impressed upon them by their experience as patients. Instead of big wards there are bedrooms for one or two patients, each of which has an outlet on to a veranda where all the sunshine available is obtained. Bright furnishings provide a most agreeable effect.

On 1 July 1934 *The Times* wrote:

PAPWORTH VILLAGE SETTLEMENT
The New Hospital
The report of the Medical Director, Sir Pendrill Varrier-Jones, states that progress is being made in many directions even more rapidly than financial considerations permit. 'To proceed further along the lines of thoracic surgery seems essential and we are providing a special 22-bed surgical block. When this is completed we shall

have at Papworth what we believe to be the most complete scheme for the treatment of tuberculosis that exists anywhere.'

On 23 July 1936 *The Times* wrote:

NEW SURGICAL HOSPITAL AT PAPWORTH
Opening by The Earl of Athlone

The tuberculosis colony at Papworth Hall was again honoured by royal visitors today when Princess Alice, Countess of Athlone, and the Earl of Athlone showed their keen interest in the work. The Earl declared the new surgical hospital open.

Sir Pendrill Varrier-Jones said that Papworth had created a record for that was the 15th visit from members of the Royal House of Windsor.

All this development was costing money, far more money than the Industries could make. In 1932 the Rt. Hon. Stanley Baldwin, MP and a Vice President of Papworth, made an appeal over the radio. Of Varrier-Jones he said: 'For years he has struggled on, entirely without endowments, harassed by the conflicting claims of finance and humanity. His humanity has won, but his overdraft is enormous.'

A high-spot in publicity was reached in December 1935 when the world premiere of the film *The Ghost Goes West* was given at the Leicester Square Theatre, attended by HM Queen Mary. Seats at prices ranging from half a guinea to ten guineas [£65 to £650 in today's money] were sold out, and the proceeds devoted to the provision of a nurses' home at Papworth. At the same performance a showing was made of the film *The Story of Papworth*.

Two years later, on 20 April 1937, Jack Payne and his band played for over 500 guests at a Festival Dinner at Grosvenor House, presided over by HRH The Duke of Kent, then President of Papworth, in the company of His Grace The Archbishop of Canterbury, The Duke of Atholl, The Marquess and Marchioness of Willingdon, Sir Patrick Hastings, KC and many other distinguished people. There cannot have been many 'right' people by this time who did not know or were not known by Sir Pendrill Varrier-Jones. His work had received recognition in the form of a knighthood in 1931.

On 21 February 1937, there was a simple celebration at Papworth to mark the 21st anniversary of the opening of the Bourn colony. As Rowland Parker noted in 1977:

For Sir Pendrill Varrier-Jones it was the proudest and most touching experience of his life. Twelve of the early patients at Bourn returned to give thanks for the part he had played in their restoration to health. And what a bevy of fit men they looked – fathers and grandfathers! – Sir Pendrill responded to the toast, but with great difficulty. It was, I presume, one of those occasions when to feel most is to say least.

The voice that had won converts to his faith throughout Europe and America; the voice that had charmed royalty and nobility; had gracefully acknowledged honours conferred upon him by the Royal College of Physicians; that voice failed him when those simple ordinary men came back to say 'thank you for saving our lives'.

He died suddenly on Jan. 30th, 1941. Sir Pendrill had lived only 57 years, but he had managed to pack into them about a hundred years' worth of distance run. To hear the old ones talk at Papworth today, you might think he was still there. In a way, I think he is.

Parker concluded:

His life was gentle and the elements
So mixed in him that Nature might stand up
And say to all the world, 'This was a man'!

Papworth Colony

This is what Varrier-Jones wrote himself on a visit to the USA in 1926:

THE WORK OF PAPWORTH COLONY
by P.C. Varrier-Jones, MA, MRCS, LRCP

I deem it a great honour to be asked to address this Conference on the work of the Papworth colony. My task is made the lighter because during my stay in America I find many friends who not only know where Papworth is, but are fully conversant with its work, its aims, its aspirations. I no longer have to answer the question: Where is Papworth? Indeed, it is almost superfluous for me to answer the question: What is Papworth?

Papworth is a Village Settlement for the Tuberculous, a community of consumptives who have learned to live with the limitations imposed upon the life of a consumptive, and even to enjoy that life.

A tuberculosis colony is a community of consumptives in which the hygienic and economic factors have been readjusted to suit the abnormal physical and mental state of its members.

Some years ago, when I was engaged in doing the work of a County Tuberculosis Officer, I was confronted with the problem of what to do with those patients who, having had a period of sanatorium treatment, were unable, on account of the extent of the disease or its only partial arrest, to pursue their previous employment. At first I followed the line of least resistance and gave plausible advice. I had been taught, and the text books were full of it, that a consumptive should obtain a light job in the open air. I reiterated this advice; I even went so far as to prescribe the requisite hours during which the patient should work. I reminded him that even during these short hours he should take great care not to over-exert himself; in short, I preached a ca'canny policy. I had been taught that a nourishing diet was absolutely essential for combating the disease; that fats preferably in the form of cream, should be liberally served, and that altogether a generous diet should most certainly be prescribed. I went further than this; I advised long periods of rest, and I particularly advised that the resting hours should be spent in a well-ventilated room, preferably facing south, the windows to be kept open and the room properly heated in inclement weather. I advised all this, and yet little success attended my efforts. The patients returned again and again for further examination and advice. They lost weight, very soon their general condition was worse than before they were sent to the sanatorium. Why did this state of affairs exist? I put the question squarely to myself, and in time I got the answer.

'How can I buy good food in abundance on 7/6d a week?' said one.

'How can I find a part-time job, when healthy men are unemployed?' said another.

'How can I rest with a young family clamouring for food?' said a third.

And I woke up to the fact that the advice I had been giving, however suitable for the well-to-do, was utterly unsuited to those with whom I had to deal – with the mass of working men and women who cannot afford to be consumptive.

Nowadays, this important aspect of the problem of tuberculosis is summed up in the term 'after-care,' but how many of us realise that after-care means much more than a dole of money and food, and the above-quoted advice, which can never be followed? How many of us recognise that we are dealing with a complex situation, in which medicine, economics, sociology and psychology are interwoven, as for various reasons they are in no other branch of our medical work. To send a man to a sanatorium, while his wife and family live on bare necessities at home, is only touching the fringe of the problem. When he returns, improved in health no doubt, but still unemployed and probably unemployable, it means that there is one more to be fed and, what is worse, that a source of infection is let loose amongst badly nourished, badly housed individuals, whose resistance to disease is already low and daily becomes lower. The 'massive' dose necessary to infect these children need, indeed, be far less massive owing to their decreased power of resistance. Is there any means of cutting this vicious circle? Is there any means of making the 'family' the unit to be dealt with? Is there any means of finding an environment wherein the sub-standard man may work, may help to support his family, and in which the danger of infection will be reduced, if not altogether removed? That is the problem Papworth is out to solve. That is the situation with which it has continuously grappled during the last ten years. By trial and error, through storm and sunshine, we have built up the Hospital, Sanatorium and Village Settlement, all working together towards the solution to the problem.

These various units are combined under one administrative head, and it is my firm conviction that a colony for the tuberculous must contain all these units, if success is to be attained.

It may be objected that a 'hospital unit' is not essential for a colony where only 'arrested' cases are admitted for treatment and training, and subsequent settlement. But, as I have pointed out elsewhere, there are very few arrested cases of pulmonary tuberculosis, and, as has been stated by the late Dr Hermann Biggs and others, if all our sanatoria admitted only incipient or early cases of pulmonary tuberculosis, not a third of the beds would be occupied. Most important of all, it must be remembered that tuberculosis is a fluctuating disease, a disease

22

in which periods of so-called arrest alternate with periods of exacerbation.

If the disease after sanatorium treatment is indeed permanently arrested (and he would be a bold physician who would make such a statement), then there is no need for after-care or a special environment and a sheltered existence. It is because permanent arrest is so seldom attained amongst the working classes, that the special environment of a village settlement becomes necessary. It is because our sanatoria are filled with cases in which no permanent arrest of the disease can be expected, because the damaged organ can function in a special environment only, that village settlements are called for. They are necessary for those very cases who find it impossible to obtain employment in the outside world, and who daily crowd into the dispensaries in our large cities, looking for a cure which never comes.

We must open our doors wide, for treatment and prevention go hand in hand. It is seldom recognised that it is possible at one and the same time to treat the disease and prevent its spread. A six months' stay in a sanatorium followed by a period of temporary arrest when the patient is able to return home and work may be one form of this combination. But when the disease re-asserts itself and the patient again becomes infectious, it is imperative that further treatment and other preventive measures should be adopted. What should these measures be? What form should they take? Should they be a further effort at temporary repair only to be broken down again, or should they be permanent treatment involving segregation?

It is often asserted that the bed-ridden case of tuberculosis is not so great a danger to the community as an infectious ambulatory case. This may well be so. Fear of infection when the patient looks ill makes for the taking of necessary precautions. There is no such fear of infection when the patient is up and about, and does not exhibit the signs of disease which we popularly associate with 'consumption'. The sputum of such a patient may be from time to time crowded with bacilli, and it is no uncommon thing to find amongst the settlers in the village that this is the case. In ordinary life this danger is there all unsuspected, and it is this danger which has to be avoided, if prevention is to be a reality. The difficulties of dealing with such a relapsing case are many, but they are not insuperable. To send the patient to a hospital for advanced cases is entirely unnecessary, for he may have many years of life before him; the depression of such surroundings will soon drive the man home. The usual patching-up in a sanatorium does not meet the case, for after each period of treatment the man is less likely to find employment than before. The crux of the question is the finding of suitable employment under sheltered conditions, with facilities for treatment whenever an exacerbation of the disease manifests itself. The worst evil, and the greatest obstacle to the recovery of the consumptive, is enforced idleness. I have from time to time stressed this point, and it is with no small satisfaction that I find my point of view vindicated by an extensive statistical investigation recently published. Residence in a village settlement holds out that hope.

If our imagination cannot rise beyond the possibility of retaining patients in an 'institution' as the only means of segregation, we may well despair. It is not only unreasonable to expect a man voluntarily to undergo restraint for an indefinite period, it is against all precedent. A life filled with monotonous routine, purposeless work, and unbounded leisure, whether for mischief or pleasure, is not to be thought of. Nor again is the continuous separation from the family to be tolerated. Both must be dismissed from our minds if we are to make our Colony a success.

If we are convinced that enforced idleness is detrimental to those in whom the disease is quiescent or partially arrested – and I think it is now agreed on all hands that this is the case – how are we going to provide suitable employment for those whose physical and mental condition cannot withstand the strain of the industrial world? If a solution can be found to this part of the problem, we are well on the way to ultimate success. We are apt to consider the question too much from the purely medical point of view. While it is generally agreed that certain trades are detrimental to consumptives, we may be condemning a great number which are really blameless *per se*. A long list of 'don'ts' is not the best encouragement with which to begin a task. It is fortunate for most of us that when we are young we are not presented with such a list – we soon learn how many they are by experience, but I suppose few of us would ever venture on Life's path if we were fully conscious of its ever-present dangers. We simply go on, experience alone teaches us, and it is the same with the employment of the tuberculous. If we took into account all the 'don'ts' of our rehabilitation schemes, we should speedily come to a standstill. Why not set out and prove by experience that what appears to be wrong may be wrong only under certain conditions, and that it is not detrimental in itself? Let me give you an illustration.

The printing trade is notorious for the large number of consumptives in its workshops. Immediately it is assumed that printing is of itself a dangerous trade for the tuberculous, that the dust from the type and the fumes from the lead are a predisposing cause of the disease. This is a plausible but erroneous idea. It is not the trade itself which is injurious, but the conditions, taken as a whole, under which it is carried on. Where are the printing shops situated? Where the tuberculous worker abounds, mostly in underground cellars. No sunlight ever penetrates those dusty caves. One coughing consumptive sprays the bacilli not only into the mouths of his fellows – they work face to face – but also into the cases of type. Nature's best disinfectant, the sun, never enters. Add to this, the vitiated atmosphere, and the soil is prepared for the growth of the tubercle bacillus.

Again, there is no wiser saying with regard to the consumptive than this: It is the pace that kills. The rush orders of the ordinary printing works, the method of employment with long hours of overtime, all these factors prepare the way for physical and mental breakdown, lowered resistance and massive infection. Is it necessary for printing to be carried on in these surroundings? The answer is obviously in the negative and with suitable organisation the rushing pace can also be modified. It has been done at Papworth, and I have repeated the experiment at Preston Hall with success. Similarly with very many other trades, some are obviously too heavy, but it is astonishing how one hard and heavy trade, agriculture, has been consistently recommended as suitable for the tuberculous. Attention has been diverted from the severity of the toil on account of our worship of the fetish 'open-air.' Fresh, wholesome, and pure air may be had in any workshop or factory, if due attention is paid to the ventilation of the building, and it is now coming to be recognised that work with less physical exertion, carried out under ideal factory conditions, can be performed by the consumptive, while heavy outdoor work cannot be performed without detriment to his health.

It is clear, therefore, that with regard to the selection of trades, we have to bear in mind the principles which underlie the employment of labour, and alter the environment to suit a damaged constitution. The smaller details will soon fit in like a jig-saw puzzle. Let us put our faith in the experimental method – a method which has in the past rewarded us so richly by results.

I cannot do more than touch upon the economic question, and I shall not attempt to go into detail, for details differ from town to town, county to county, country to country. But certain underlying principles soon present themselves. Our experiences at Papworth to test the conditions under which men will remain in the country, although used to town life, and not town life only, but London life, are highly instructive. Our experience is – as we have all along reiterated – that the first great question to be considered is that of a wage or payment for work done. The Colony can and does offer good conditions of work, conditions that involve no impairment of a man's self-respect; the Colony offers chances of promotion, chances which are lacking in the outside world to a sub-standard man. Instead of being pushed against the wall by the competition of the healthy worker, he is given the opportunity of making good without the inferiority complex working its will. The disease from which he suffers is already a sufficient handicap, without our adding to it the struggle of competition in which the odds are all against him.

We have heard *ad nauseam* that the consumptive will not work, but when we hear such a statement, investigation usually proves that he is either up against overwhelming odds in the shape of a 'healthy foreman or manager,' or that the management is hopelessly incapable. Most of our schemes for the employment of the consumptive break down on account of inefficient management, or on account of that lack of sympathetic understanding occasioned by looking at him through medical spectacles, and neglecting to put on our human glasses.

How many of us have ever thought about a consumptive's aspirations and desires? He does not believe that his days are numbered, and it is our duty not to undeceive him. By providing any avenue of approach to better material conditions we must assist the man to work out his own salvation. We must do this by means of our guidance and our ability to provide that environment in which his salvation lies. I wish especially to emphasise this aspect of the work. All the emphasis I am able to exert seems feeble compared with the importance which it ought to have. Let me give one final illustration; I will leave it to you to fill in the gaps.

In starting colonies it has been the rule to set up an industry and then find the men to run it. No success is attained that way. First find your man, encourage him and build up your business round him. The touchstone of success is personality. Without the spirit of adventure and personal endeavour our work is like 'sounding brass and a tinkling cymbal.' All the industries at Papworth were built round individual men. It is their energy and foresight which has brought success. It matters not what trade it may be; the very disability of the men who run it will point the way for the readjustments demanded by their condition. Your large businesses did not start full grown in the palatial skyscrapers I saw as I entered New York harbour. Many of them bear the names of those who started in a small way of business. The maxim therefore for the industries of village settlements should be: The man first, the industry afterwards. Let the doctor efface himself, and be content to be the power behind the throne, the buffer between the sheltered environment and the competition of the outside world. The village settlement is a community, not an institution, and a community of sub-standard men making good.

I will close by quoting Dr Hermann Biggs, whose skill in preventive medicine led him to make the following prophecy in 1910:

'What is needed is an industrial colony where proper occupations can be provided under proper conditions, with proper living quarters where "arrested" cases can earn a livelihood and maintain their health. I believe such an industrial colony once established could be made self-supporting, but a large fund would be required for the erection of houses and sanitary workshops and the construction of the business of such a colony. The future will probably see the solution of this.'

Achievements of a great man

Tragically, as we have seen, Sir Pendrill Varrier-Jones died suddenly in January 1941 at the relatively young age of 57. This was his obituary by Humphrey Rolleston:

SIR PENDRILL VARRIER-JONES

On 30 January 1941, when in good health and spirits and apparently quite recovered from an influenzal attack early in the month, Sir Pendrill Charles Varrier-Jones died at Papworth within half an hour after the onset of a sudden heart seizure. Thus to the last he was actively devoted to the Papworth Village Settlement which he had organized as an economic and social continuation of the tuberculosis sanatorium. He was the pioneer of the colony system for the tuberculous in which, when patients have so far improved as the result of sanatorium and other treatment that the disease is well on the way to be arrested, they continue to live under medical supervision and begin to work and so to earn a living wage. Otherwise in the past tuberculous patients on leaving a sanatorium were generally obliged to return to the environment where the disease began, and to the unequal competition with vigorous rivals for a living; this is often responsible for a relapse and acceleration on the downward path. At first this conception shared the fate of other advances now thoroughly orthodox; some authorities, though admitting that it was an ideal, regarded it as visionary and financially impossible. It was Varrier-Jones's achievement to prove that it could be successfully accomplished.

He was born on 24 February 1883, as the only son of the late Dr Charles Morgan Jones and Margaret Varrier of Glyn Taff, Troedyrhiw, Glamorgan, and had one sister. Educated at Epsom College, and Wycliffe College, Stonehouse, Glos., of which he later became President, he was a Foundation Scholar at Cambridge and was placed in the first class of Part I of the Natural Sciences Tripos 1905 and in the second class of Part II in the next year. Then entering the medical school of St Bartholomew's Hospital he qualified MRCS, LRCP in 1910 and was house physician during the following year. Returning to Cambridge as a research worker under Sir German Sims Woodhead, Professor of Pathology, he investigated the continuous temperature by a self-recording instrument previously devised by Arthur Gamgee. While acting as temporary tuberculosis officer for Cambridgeshire he became painfully conscious of the incongruity and futility of giving the routine advice to 'get a light job in the open air and have three good nourishing meals a day', which poor patients can very rarely carry out. Accordingly in 1915 he opened, at first with one patient in a shelter, the

Cambridgeshire Tuberculosis Colony at Bourn. Three years later this colony, then with twenty-five patients, moved to Papworth Hall, twelve miles from Cambridge, formerly the property of Hooley, the financier.

In the early days the difficulties, especially of finance, were many and serious but his enthusiasm and organizing ability won him the encouragement of Sir Robert Morant, Sir Frederick Milner, 'the soldiers' and sailors' friend', who interested the Royal family in Papworth, and of Sir Ernest Cassel who most generously helped in the move to Papworth. Sir Clifford Allbutt and Sir German Sims Woodhead gave their support by collaboration with Varrier-Jones in publications between 1915 and 1925, showing the limitations, such as waste of time and money, of tuberculosis sanatoriums and dispensaries alone, and explaining the value of the Papworth scheme as an addition to the after-care of the tuberculous. Sir James Kingston Fowler in his obiter dicta, such as 'the working man cannot afford the time to be an early case of pulmonary tuberculosis', 'a light occupation in the open air is seldom found', 'a tuberculosis dispensary that has become a tuberculin dispensary has become a very dangerous place', expressed some of Varrier-Jones's principles.

During twenty-two years expansion was continuous and intensive at Papworth. The population of the colony is now 1,200; of these 500 – men, women, and nurses – are ill and in new hospitals. No tuberculous applicant, whatever the state of the disease – early or advanced – is ever refused admission on that score. Sanatorium treatment is provided in 100 chalets until the occupants are well enough to be transferred to the hostels where single men and women at work in the Papworth workshops are lodged; and there are 141 model cottages occupied by ex-patients with their families. Of the 122 children born in the colony all are free from tuberculosis, thus meeting any suggestion that a tuberculosis colony is certain to be an infective focus of endemic tuberculosis. Varrier-Jones took a far wider view of the control of tuberculosis than the purely medical; he paid special attention to the patients' economic needs which often, on account of disability, become acute, and with understanding sympathy for the mental anxiety about the financial state of their families and dependants arranged a psychological clinic, just as he provided for their physical requirements at Papworth, for example by a surgical unit under J.B. Hunter, and an X-ray department. The economic and psychological factors were thus important in the organization of the village settlement for the tuberculous. Constantly on the watch for advances, he instituted research laboratories with a Bulletin. As recently as January 1941 he was actively preparing the ground for an undergraduate school of tuberculosis at Papworth.

He was most courageous, and some indeed thought rash, in financial matters; thus when extensions appeared necessary he started them whether or not funds were available to meet the cost. Eventually he always made good, especially in connection with the phenomenal success of the Papworth industries, the sales of which increased from year to year, reaching fresh records in 1939 and 1940. But in the early period there was the question of payment for raw material before the fine products of the Papworth workshops could be made and sold. This was accommodated by an overdraft at the bank, and when warned about its mounting height he seemed to comfort himself by the remark that he 'might really be driven to remove his overdraft in a taxi to the nearest bank'. The most important practical features of the Papworth scheme are the industries and workshops, which solve the economic difficulty by enabling ex-patients and convalescents to work for a living under the Trade Union rate of wages and under medical supervision. As the founder and administrator of the Papworth industries Varrier-Jones showed a business capacity rare indeed, especially among members of the medical fraternity. A shrewd judge of character, he chose his assistants, trusted and inspired them with his ideals for many years; thus Miss K.L. Borne has been matron since 1915, and Dr L.B. Stott a medical officer from 1921.

At the time of his death he had reached the highest point in his career, though he did not consider that his labours were nearly completed; he might have echoed Rhodes's last recorded words: 'So little done: so much to do.' His work has been widely recognized, for many pilgrims from abroad visited the Mecca of tuberculosis after-care at Papworth, which has been copied in this country at Preston Hall near Maidstone, at Barrowmore Hall near Chester, in Eire at Peamount near Dublin, in the United States at the Potts Memorial hospital at Livingston, New York, and in France by the village settlement at Salagnac. He visualized a great expansion of the Papworth model, and was always glad to advise similar colonies for subnormal men, and did so at Enham (now allied with Papworth), of which he was honorary medical director, at Preston Hall, and at Peamount. He received the honour of knighthood in 1931, was appointed president in 1932 of a new international body formed for special and intensive study of the after-care of the tuberculous, which is affiliated with the Union internationale contre la Tuberculose, and would have represented the Government at Berlin in 1939 at the meeting of the Union internationale contre la Tuberculose, arranged for September 1939. At the Royal College of Physicians of London he was elected a Fellow in 1934, had delivered the Mitchell Lecture on tuberculosis in 1927, taking village settlements for the tuberculous as his subject, and in 1939 was awarded the Weber-Parkes Prize for tuberculosis.

He was a truly great man, the like of whom we can hardly hope to see again; he set a wonderful example of whole-hearted devotion to the good work he organized and has left for others to continue.

This is what Ben Milstein, of whom we shall read much more later, said of Varrier-Jones:

Varrier-Jones's achievement was not a new method of treatment. Open air treatment had been practised by Bodington at Sutton Coldfield as long ago as 1840, and the first open air wards at the Brompton Hospital were established in 1899. What became obvious to him was

35

that the family and not the patient was the individual unit. Varrier-Jones's master-stroke was to save the families from penury, because a diagnosis of tuberculosis meant that the breadwinner was no longer able to work and the family was ruined. By putting the patients to work and paying them, Varrier-Jones guaranteed that the families could survive. However, his greatest success was undoubtedly the concept of rehabilitation and he could certainly never have realised the full consequences of this himself. At the time when he established his method the victims of the First World War were begging in the streets of all the major cities in England and no attempt was being made to restore them to a useful place in the community or to enable them to make the best of life in spite of their handicaps.

Chapter 2

THE POST-WAR WORLD

Progress after the war
The National Health Service
Christopher Parish
Steps towards open-heart surgery
Ben Milstein
The Heart–Lung Machine Department
Background to cardiology at Papworth
Cardiac catheterisation and the X-ray Department

Progress after the war

Fortunately the development at Papworth did not grind to a halt with the sudden death of Sir Pendrill Varrier-Jones. Air Commodore R.R. Trail succeeded him as Medical Director. He had been serving as a consultant physician. Treatment for those suffering from tuberculosis continued and the hospital adapted itself to the National Health Service Act of 1946. In 1951 more than 120 men and women were admitted to the hospital from all over the country. Varrier-Jones had often travelled to Europe and North America and in subsequent years doctors from overseas came to Papworth to learn from what was being done there.

In 1935 a surgical block of 28 beds had been opened. The Duke of Gloucester laid the foundation stone. These were several of the surgical operations carried out in 1937:

Phrenic crush	5
Thoracoplasty	8
Thorascopy – starving the lung of oxygen to kill off TB	7
Bronchoscopy	4
Extrapleural pneumothorax	3
Rib resection	3
Miscellaneous	9

Over the following ten years between 40 and 70 operations a year were performed. In 1943 five thoracotomies were performed.

Because of his increasing commitments at King's College Hospital, where he ultimately became Dean,

J.B. Hunter resigned from the staff of Papworth Hospital in 1945, and O.S. Tubbs was appointed. He was the first specialist surgeon on the staff of the hospital. He was at this time thoracic surgeon to St Bartholomew's Hospital and also to the Brompton Hospital, and he had promised that if the opportunity arose, he would take on the surgery at Papworth. Under his management the number of surgical operations increased.

In 1946 Tubbs performed the first lung removal operation at Papworth. He resigned in 1947 because of reactivation of tuberculosis which he had acquired in 1943. In that year Kent Harrison was appointed as the first full-time thoracic surgeon. The work slowly increased, although operating sessions were held only twice a week. Surgical treatment was now regarded as both respectable and successful and a two-year waiting list had developed. However, any increase in the throughput was continually restricted by the difficulty of recruiting adequate numbers of nursing staff.

In fact nearly all the junior nurses were ex-patients, the theatre sister had a thoracoplasty and the Matron had to act as runner in the operating theatre. Kent Harrison described this situation as a nightmare.

In 1947 Ian English was appointed as the first consultant anaesthetist. He was joined in 1952 by Robert Loder, who had worked intermittently at Papworth since 1948. Loder remembered encountering the Deputy Medical Superintendent, Dr Stott, who was a very eccentric man, listening to the trunk of a tree with a stethoscope. He was murmuring to himself, 'This tree is getting very old'.

In fact J.B. Hunter continued to visit Papworth in a

consultative capacity after Tubbs was appointed, and acted as locum tenens after Tubbs resigned. He did not finally sever his connection with the hospital until 1949.

In 1944 Professor Gabriel Waksman had made the important discovery of the antibiotic Streptomycin, which killed off the need for surgery for tuberculosis. It was not realised at the time that this drug could be curative. It was given in too large doses and serious toxic effects were encountered. Para-aminosalicylic acid was synthesised in 1946, and Isoniazid in 1952. Surgeons were quick to realise that these drugs could be used to prevent the dreaded complications of lung resection for tuberculosis, namely bronchopleural fistula and spread of the disease to other parts of the lung. With a short period of antibiotic cover, resection could be made safe and it became increasingly used.

The National Health Service

A very important development in the history of Papworth Hospital, indeed of every hospital in the United Kingdom, was the establishment of the National Health Service or NHS as it became known.

There is no doubt that the first half of the 20th century was a very difficult period for the majority of the British people. Even before the outbreak of the First World War in 1914 there was a decade of rising inflation leading to a growing number of strikes by workers only beginning to feel the benefits of trade unions. The war, originally known as the Great War, far from being over by Christmas 1914, ran on to November 1918 with 37 million deaths around the world, including nearly a million British.

This was followed by two decades of economic hardship with high unemployment and extreme poverty for millions of people. Finally, there was another world war with over 60 million deaths.

The majority of British people were determined that there should be a change and, in spite of the fact that they gave credit to the Conservative Party leader, Winston Churchill, for winning the Second World War, in 1945 they voted in the Labour Party which promised reforms aimed at producing a more equal society.

In retrospect, as Boris Johnson points out in his book, *The Churchill Factor*, Churchill deserves some credit both for what became known as the Welfare State and for appointing William Beveridge, whose 1942 report on *Social Insurance and Allied Services*, known as the Beveridge Report, was the influential document leading to the social reforms of the Labour government led by Prime Minister Clement Attlee from 1945 to 1950.

Beveridge identified five 'Giant Evils' in British Society. These were squalor, ignorance, want, idleness and disease. His report proposed widespread reform to tackle these evils.

The Labour Party, voted into power in 1945, adopted the Beveridge proposals and passed a number of revolutionary acts – the Family Allowances Act 1945, National Insurance (Industrial Injuries) Act 1946, National Insurance Act 1946, National Health Service Act 1946, Pensions (Increase) Act 1947, Landlord and Tenant (Rent Control) Act 1949, and National Insurance Acts in 1948 and 1949.

Clement Attlee appointed Aneurin Bevan as Minister of Health, giving him the responsibility for creating a new comprehensive National Health Service. As Bevan himself said:

> The collective principle asserts that … no society can legitimately call itself civilised if a sick person is denied medical aid because of lack of means.

On an appointed day, 5 July 1948, having overcome opposition from the Conservative Party and even sections of the Labour Party and from the British Medical Association, Bevan's National Health Service Act of 1946 came into force. Some 2,688 voluntary and municipal hospitals in England and Wales were nationalised and came under Bevan's supervisory control as Health Minister.

Bevan said:

> This is the biggest single experiment in social service that the world has ever seen undertaken.

The creation of the National Health Service, which Beveridge thought essential to his wider vision, was not easy to set up. Britain had had a system of voluntary hospitals, raising their own cash, which varied greatly in size, efficiency and cleanliness. Later, it also had municipal hospitals, many growing out of the original workhouses. Some of these in go-ahead cities like London, Birmingham or Nottingham, were efficient, modern places whose beds were generally kept for the poor. Others were squalid. Money for the voluntary hospitals came from investments, gifts, charity events, payments and a hotchpotch of insurance schemes. Today we think of ward closures and hospitals on the edge of bankruptcy as diseases of the NHS. The pre-war system was much less certain and wards closed for lack of funds then too.

By the time the war ended, most of Britain's hospitals had been brought into a single national emergency medical service. The question was what should happen now – should they be nationalised or allowed back to go their own way? A similar question mark hung over family doctors. GPs depended on private fees, though most of them also took poor patients through some kind of health insurance scheme. When not working from home or a surgery, they would often double up operating in municipal hospitals where, as non-specialists, they sometimes hacked away incompetently. And the insurance system excluded many elderly people, housewives and children, who were therefore put off visiting the doctor at all, unless they were in the greatest pain or the gravest danger. The situation was similar with dentistry and optical services, which were not available to anyone without the cash to pay for them. Out of this Labour was determined to provide the first system of medical care, free at the point of need, that there had been in any Western democracy.

Simplicity is a great weapon. Nye Bevan's single biggest decision was to take all the hospitals, the voluntary ones and the ones run by local councils, into a single nationalised system. It would have regional boards but it would all come under the Ministry of Health in London. This was heroic self-confidence. For the first time, a single politician would take ultimate responsibility for every public hospital in the

44

land. Herbert Morrison, the great defender of municipal power, was against this nationalisation but was brushed aside by Bevan.

A more dangerous enemy by far were the hospital doctors. What followed was the most important, most difficult domestic fight of the post-war Labour government's life. The doctors, organised under the Conservative-leaning leadership of the British Medical Association, had it in their power to stop the NHS dead in its tracks by simply refusing to work for it. They were worried about their standing in the new system – would they be mere state functionaries? And they were suspicious of Bevan, quite rightly. He had wanted to have the doctors nationalised too, all employed by the state, all paid by the state, with no private fees allowed. This would mean a war with the very men and women trusted by millions to cure and care for them. But Bevan, the red-hot socialist, turned out to be a realist and diplomatist. He began by wooing the top hospital doctors, the consultants. The physicians and surgeons were promised they could keep their lucrative pay beds and private practice. Bevan later admitted that he had 'stuffed their mouths with gold'. Next he retreated on the payment of the 50,000 GPs, promising they could continue being paid on the basis of how many people they were treating, rather than getting a flat salary. This wasn't enough. In a poll of doctors, for everyone who said he would work in the new National Health Service, nine said they we would refuse to take part.

As the day for the official beginning of the NHS drew closer and there was a tense political stand-off, Bevan continued to offer concessions while also attacking the doctors' leaders as 'a small body of politically poisoned people' sabotaging the will of Parliament. Would the old Britain of independent professionals, with their cliques, status and fees, accept the new Britain of state control? They did, of course. More concessions and more threats brought them round, in the end. Bevan was backed by a Parliamentary majority and they were not. But it had been a long, tight, nasty battle.

When the NHS opened for business on 5 July 1948, there was a flood of people to surgeries, hospitals and chemists. Fifteen months later, Bevan announced that 5.25 million pairs of free spectacles had been supplied, as well as 187 million free prescriptions. By then, 8.5 million people had already had free dental treatment. Almost immediately there were complaints about the cost and extravagance, the surge of demand for everything from dressings to wigs. There was much anecdotal evidence of waste and misuse. There certainly was waste. The new bureaucracy was cumbersome. And it is possible to overestimate the change – most people had had access to some kind of affordable healthcare before the NHS, though it was patchy and working-class women had a particular difficulty in getting treatment. But the most important thing it did was to take away fear. Before it, millions at the bottom of the pile had suffered untreated hernias, cancers, toothache, ulcers and all kinds of illness, rather than face the humiliation and worry of being unable to afford treatment. There are many moving accounts of the queues of unwell, impoverished people surging forward for treatment in the early days of the NHS, arriving in hospitals and doctors' waiting rooms for the first time not as beggars but as citizens with a sense of right. If there was one single domestic good that the British took from the sacrifices of the war, it was a health service free at the point of use. We have clung to it tenaciously ever since and no mainstream party has dared suggest taking it away.

The introduction of the National Health Act allowed Papworth to expand its activities in helping patients to build up their work rate, so that patients could come to Papworth and increase their time working gradually from three hours a day to six. A positive sputum sample was not a bar to admission. In fact it was considered one of the best reasons for admission. Papworth, because it was also a sanatorium, could offer earlier training than other centres.

Christopher Parish

A very important contributor to the development of Papworth Hospital in the second half of the 20th century was Christopher Parish. He was the first cardiothoracic surgeon at Papworth. He was appointed in 1952 as the thoracic surgeon, and this is what he wrote about the hospital at the time:

> I recall that at that time Papworth was a very tiny organisation surgically, a little, tiny theatre – with an even smaller anaesthetic room – and very few facilities, and certainly not enough to do modern thoracic surgery. As a result, I made it a condition of my appointment that I was to get new operating theatres. I decided that

it was a good idea to develop cardiothoracic surgery in Cambridge, as there were no facilities of any note. There was a visiting surgeon and two visiting physicians from London. It was done on a very peripatetic basis. It was mainly tuberculosis lung, or carcinoma lung, or a certain amount of oesophageal surgery, but I'd had experience during the war with all types of surgery with the 8th Army in the desert, in the Salerno landing and again at Anzio, where we had to deal with all sorts of chest wounds, and through Italy to the Po Valley battle, and finally to Verona. Amongst these cases, there was one, a German prisoner of war, who had a large piece of British shrapnel sticking out of his chest wall and projecting in to the left ventricle of the heart. With the use of two chromic catgut sutures and big curved intestinal needles, and in the absence of ethical committees and families to consult, we decided to go ahead and attempt to remove it. We had a living patient. We had plenty of blood because the soldiers were always willing to give blood.

By allowing a lot of blood to escape, but no air to enter, we managed to close this wound in the heart and the patient survived. That was my first example of cardiac surgery and I knew you could operate on the heart. Howard Florey had brought Penicillin to us in Tripoli and we used it as a powder in wounds at Salerno in September 1943.

The teaching that I had been given as a student was that 'any surgeon who attempted to suture a wound of the heart would lose the respect of his colleagues'. So it wasn't surprising that because I knew it could be done,

I decided we ought to try and develop cardiac surgery with thoracic surgery at Papworth. We knew that TB was under control, the new antibiotics had come in, the case material was falling away but there were lots of cardiac cases waiting to be done, even dying on the waiting list. The initial opposition was chiefly by the nursing staff. However, we persevered and the Regional Board supported us.

Unlike modern surgeons, we hadn't got trained cardiac and pump technicians. Before the construction of the twin operating theatres with space to accommodate all the equipment round the theatre, we had to do all that ourselves. In the past the theatres were more or less standard, you had room for an anaesthetic trolley, for a nurse's kit, and so on, and the main operating table and the anaesthetic machine but nothing else material there. There was a lot of travelling, and the A14 hadn't yet been developed so we had to meander through the villages to get to Ipswich. Dr Grove, from Norwich, was doing a certain amount of TB surgery at Foxhall Hospital at Ipswich. I alternated with him to start with and did some surgery there, but eventually he took over all the Ipswich operating. With the help of the Ministry of Health, we managed to get Dr Lum appointed at Papworth as the first consultant respiratory physiologist in the country. The Ministry was very helpful in many ways. When we were considering getting the new theatres established, Iain Macleod, who was then Minister of Health, came one day and I saw him in the anaesthetic room after I'd done a particularly gory operation. I had a lot of blood all over my shirt, and was sweating. Iain Macleod sat down and we talked and the following day we got the go ahead.

I was given the opportunity to develop Papworth from a small tuberculosis sanatorium by expanding its staffing. We had no radiologist originally. I did the first aortagrams myself with Edmund Groves (a former Sydney under-graduate), the only radiographer who was there. We had two visiting London physicians and no cardiologist. I had the job of convincing the Regional Board that we should have a cardiologist because they thought that Dr Cole, who was on the staff of Addenbrooke's, was the cardiolo-gist for the area, but he was not prepared to do the cardiac catheters and the sort of work we wanted at Papworth. Eventually we appointed Dr Fleming from Australia, and from then on the Cardiac Medical Unit developed.

The challenge was to convince people that these things were possible, that it wasn't meddlesome surgery, and that ethically it was satisfactory. I talked to various ethi-cal medical committees on the subject. The Westminster Presbyterian Training College in Cambridge held a forum on the ethics of cardiac surgery and I talked to them about it.

The Authorities also had to be convinced that car-diac surgery should be done in the country as opposed to the town, but the neurosurgeons had nowhere to go when they were appointed and they were subsequently given the first unit. So we were delayed, and for fifteen years, they've said, 'In fifteen years, you'll move in'. Even to this day, they still say, 'They want you to come into Cambridge', but we didn't want to go; the facilities at

Pendrill Varrier-Jones, the founder of Papworth Hospital.

Varrier-Jones with patients outside Papworth Hall.

The visit of Queen Mary.

HRH Queen Mary with Varrier-Jones on a visit to Papworth Village Settlement.

Varrier-Jones with a microscope.

The lake, Papworth Hall in the 1930s.

Bernhard Baron Hospital, Papworth.

Three patients at
Papworth.

Patient hut at
Papworth with
a plaque reading
'Given by her friends
in memory of Sarah
Treversian Prideaux
1853–1933'.

Papworth Colony – the chalets.

Nurses at Papworth.

Two patients in South Park.

HRH the Duchess of York,
later Queen Elizabeth, with
Pendrill Varrier-Jones on a
visit to Papworth.

Patients and staff on Baron Balcony.

Patients and a nurse sitting by the lake outside the Princess Hospital for Women at Papworth.

Two male patients in a hut in South Park.

TB patients in their huts.

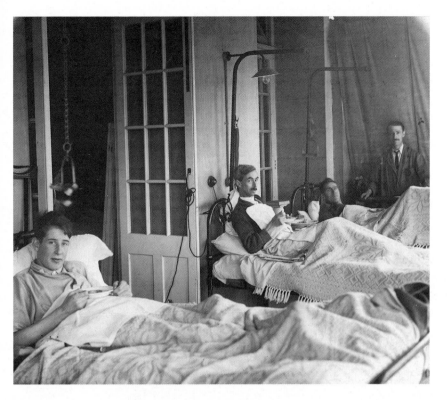

TB patients.

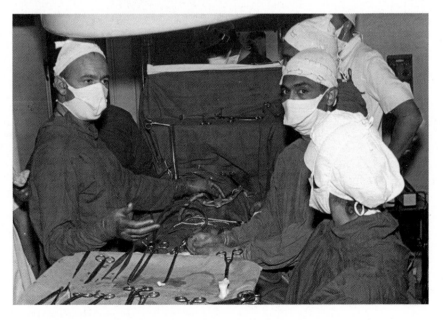

Ben Milstein in surgery at Papworth in the 1960s.

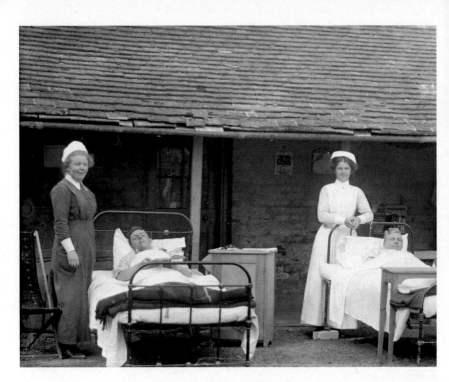

Nurses with patients.

Patient in a profound
hypothermia surface
cooling bath, used
during the first open-
heart surgeries, at
Papworth in 1958.

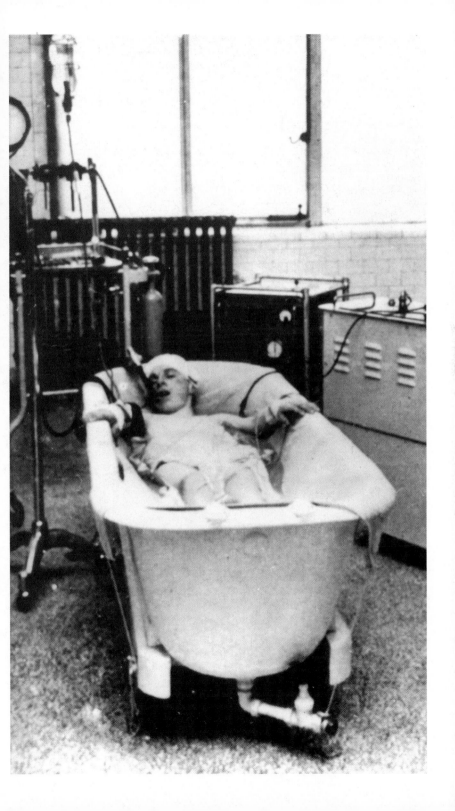

Cabinet minister
Aneurin Bevan
visits Papworth
in the 1940s.

The Duke of Gloucester
visits Papworth.

Cambridge Evening News

SPECIAL EDITION

½ PRICE
REST-O-FIRM
Single size
2 Drawer Divan
List price
£149.99 £74.99

THE BELFAST
36 ST. ANDREWS STREET,
CAMBRIDGE. Tel: 59606.

MONDAY, JANUARY 15, 1979   No 27,754   Price 6p

Talks on soccer hooligans

Britain's first major conference concerning the growing problem of soccer hooliganism was held at Ipswich today.

Among those attending the day-long discussions were representatives from all bodies affected by mis-

behaving fans. They include magistrates, licensees, referees, players, British Rail and supporters' clubs, along with police chiefs, MPs and Football League managers and chairmen.

The conference was organised by the Save Soccer action group. Chairman Alan McCosker, an Ipswich businessman, said: "We plan to

discuss a wide range of topics relating to the whole problem of violence at football grounds.

"We do not intend the conference to be simply a platform for individuals to air their views. We expect to formulate strong recommendations which will be put to Denis Howell, the Minister of Sport."

Two months ago the group circulated throughout the country a detailed charter outlining suggestions to overcome hooliganism. The proposals formed the basis for today's discussions, and included such things as the instance by, and responsibility of, players and referees. The legal right of the fans was another issue.

Mrs Mary Whitehouse

Children 'will see adult films'

Mrs Mary Whitehouse has protested that uncut "adult" continental films, beginning on BBC 2 on Friday, could be seen by more than 50 per cent of the seven to 14-year-olds in Britain.

In a letter to Mr Ian Trethowan, on behalf of the National Viewers and Listeners' Association, she has reminded the BBC's Director General of research that showed that 8 per cent of seven to 10-year-olds and 42

rain uiry

...quiry into the train ...morning, in which 12 ...t happened when a ...n into the back of a

...ned this morning that ...offering first aid, and ...their own baggage to ...kesman said that first ...engers.

...7).

...erefore the price of the ...es" will be increased to ...rom today. This is still ...s, but still, we believe, ...l value. Proof of this is ...current sales record, ...h is very close to our ...al average circulation ...,000.

paper

...around 100 pickets out- ...the newspaper's offices ...orporation Street. Cov- ...He had seen banners ...Cambridge NUJ. ...e "Evening Telegraph" ...been produced normally, ...the "News" during the

FIRST HEART TRANSPLANT AT PAPWORTH

The first UK heart transplant operation outside London took place at Papworth Hospital yesterday.

A medical bulletin issued by the hospital today stated: "The patient has had a good night and everything is proceeding smoothly."

Neither the patient nor the donor of the heart have been named by the hospital authorities. The statement on the operation by the hospital disclosed that the patient with a new heart is a 44-year-old

lasted for seven hours and was conducted by a team of heart surgeons based at Papworth and Addenbrooke's hospital Cambridge. The team leader was the consultant cardio-thoracic surgeon at Papworth hospital, Mr Terence English, who today was back in the operating theatre dealing with other patients.

Suggestions that heart transplants might be carried out in Cambridgeshire were discussed by doctors and hospital administrators as long ago as 1974. At that time Addenbrooke's Hospital, Cambridge, had already become established as one of Britain's foremost

Cambridge Evening News front page, 15 January 1979.

Papworth are better than we would get in Addenbrooke's, far better parking, far better surrounds, the patients come from all over the country and it's easier to get to Papworth than it is to get into Cambridge.

The Surgical Unit was enlarged by the addition of another wing in 1955, bringing the complement of beds up to 40. The new wing was brought into operation on 6 March 1957 and officially opened by the Duchess of Kent on 2 March 1960.

The expanded workload soon became too much for one man, and Ben Milstein was fortunate enough to be appointed as the second surgeon, with a particular interest in the development of cardiac surgery. When he arrived at Papworth on 1 January 1958, he found that there was no specialist cardiologist and no cardiological investigation service. There was one radiologist, Dr Duncan Gregg, who had been appointed in 1956. The two part-time anaesthetists both lived 30 miles away and there was no resident anaesthetic registrar. He had no secretary and no office.

The junior staff consisted of one senior registrar and one registrar. The senior registrar was a great huntsman. There was no method of trapping, chasing, snaring or hooking a wild creature with which he was not familiar. He gained the devotion of the patients when they would see him in the afternoons throwing bread pellets to the drakes on the lake. 'Ah', they would say, 'Even when he is not looking after us he finds time to look after the poor birds.' What they did not know was that each bread pellet contained a capsule of Nembutal and that after dusk, when they were all in bed, he would creep down to the lakeside, having first ensured that there would be sufficient wind to bring the birds into the bank, whence he would bundle the sleepy victims into a sack to end up in his deep freeze. He subsequently had a successful career as a flying surgeon in Queensland, but for some time after he left Papworth, he was not replaced.

The registrar's name was Sochocky but he was always known as Socky. He was a Pole who had been taken prisoner by the Russians. He had escaped and after incredible privations had arrived in the West, having walked most of the way from Russia to Italy. He was an extremely cultured man, with an appropriate quotation from Horace or Catullus, Aristotle or Dante to cover every situation. However, his English left a good deal to be desired.

Socky had an endearing habit of chewing a whole clove of garlic whenever he had a headache, which was often. As he frequently assisted Ben Milstein in the operating theatre, the overpowering aroma was a decisive stimulus to the early conclusion of the procedure. To Socky, Milstein owed the short cuts in operating which he adopted in order to reach fresh air in the shortest possible time. It was not easy to become comfortable with procedures involving the passing of long needles blind into the chest.

Steps towards open-heart surgery

Developments in this field had been followed with increasing enthusiasm by the Papworth consultants and, in November 1956, Christopher Parish and Ian English, with the aid of a grant from the Regional Hospital Board, went to Minneapolis to study C. Walton Lillehei's methods. On 17 December 1956 they began experimental surgery on pigs at the Veterinary School in Cambridge – operations that continued intermittently throughout 1957. Later that year, Dr Ian Glynn, a graduate physiologist, subsequently Professor of Membrane Physiology in the University of Cambridge, was appointed as a part-time research assistant. All this work was funded by the East Anglian Regional Hospital Board.

Papworth's two chest physicians, Dr Martin Greenberg and Dr Michael Cheffins, went to the Brompton Hospital in London to learn how to measure pressures in the heart chambers through veins to perform right heart catheterisation. There they would cool the patient down in a cold bath to stop the heart for fifteen minutes. If it was longer than that, the patient would suffer brain damage. The operation could take all day. The techniques learned at the Brompton Hospital were a great help but their experience was necessarily limited, and sometimes too trusting an acceptance of their results landed Milstein with some difficult problems on the operating table.

The theatre staff were not familiar with any forms of open-heart surgery but fortunately, in June 1958, Milstein was joined by Charles Hubbard, who had been a charge nurse in the operating theatres at the Brompton Hospital and who took charge of the theatres at Papworth. With his help they were able to start open-heart surgery using the superficial hypothermia technique – immersion in cold water. (Nowadays, the cold bath is not necessary as the patient would be put on a heart–lung machine.) The first case, a large atrial septal defect, was dealt with on 30 September 1958. Milstein had reason to remember this date because it was his birthday. In celebration of this, at the end of the operation the whole team seized him and plunged him in his theatre clothes into the bath. They had very decently emptied this and refilled it with warm water!

To overcome some of the difficulties involved in cardiac catheterisation they introduced all the direct methods of puncture of the heart chambers, including through the lungs and through the neck as well as through the chest. In these ways it was possible to obtain pressures in different parts of the heart. During that year, 1958, the first operations were carried out at Papworth on the major blood vessels on the chest outside the heart. Also the first operations on the valves in a beating heart were performed, as well as some palliative operations for children born with congenital heart diseases.

During the course of the year Milstein discovered that there were no surgeons in East Anglia treating peripheral vascular disease, with the exception of Alan Burt in Norwich. Although Milstein had had no experience in this field, he was very familiar with the surgery of the supra-diaphragmatic aorta and it seemed to him that peripheral vascular surgery would be the same only smaller. He soon discovered that there was an enormous unsatisfied demand here, which was saved from becoming an insuperable burden only by the gradual arrival of the new generation of general surgeons, most of whom practised and developed the special vascular surgery as a part of their routine activities in the 1970s.

As we have seen, a consultant cardiologist, Dr Hugh Fleming, was appointed and arrived in December 1959. Milstein had worked with him previously at the Brompton Hospital and had been very keen to get him back from Melbourne in Australia, where he was engaged in full-time cardiac catheterisation.

Milstein felt he could not overemphasise the value of the co-operations obtained from Dr Fleming and the two anaesthetists, Dr Ian English and Dr Robert Loder. The latter two spent long hours in the operating theatre helping with the medical and respiratory aspects of restarting hearts that simply would not function. Fleming too took much of the responsibility off Milstein's shoulders. He was frequently in the operating theatre sharing the problems and providing a great deal of support, especially when things went wrong.

Throughout 1958 in the attempts to develop the use of a heart–lung machine they were able to carry out experimental surgery on dogs and pigs at the School of Veterinary Medicine in Cambridge. They worked in a gardener's hut in the grounds, and later on in the post mortem room, both freezing places to work in winter.

By early 1960 they were recording survivors consistently after perfusion (in physiology, perfusion is the process of a body delivering blood to a capillary bed in its biological tissue) with the Melrose heart–lung machine. The first operation at Papworth using the heart–lung machine took place on 18 May 1960. The procedure was to close a hole in the collecting chambers of the heart.

Ben Milstein

On 22 April 2013, Ben Milstein died at the age of 94. Much of his achievement for Papworth was in the post-war period and it is appropriate to note those achievements here. His colleague, Professor John Wallwork CBE, wrote this obituary which was published in *The Guardian*:

Ben Milstein, who has died aged 94, was at the forefront of cardiothoracic surgery in the UK. On his 40th birthday, in 1958, he performed the first ever open-heart surgery, at Papworth hospital, Cambridgeshire, on a woman who had an atrial septal defect, or hole in the heart. The anaesthetised patient had been immersed in a bath of iced water before surgery so that her heart would stop beating; Ben had 10 minutes to complete the operation before brain damage occurred, which he did successfully. After its conclusion, Ben was thrown into the bath to mark the day. Forty years later, the same patient joined him to celebrate that anniversary.

Ben's first operation at Papworth was a mitral valvotomy, an operation designed to relieve heart failure as a result of a narrowed valve. He stuck his forefinger into the beating heart to stretch open the valve knowing, at that time, the procedure carried an 80 per cent risk of mortality, but his patient survived. In 1962, Ben replaced an aortic valve – again, a novel procedure. This was a time of brave men performing brave operations on brave patients. It is difficult to imagine the excitement and energy of those risky, innovative times now that cardiac surgery has become relatively routine and safe.

After the Second World War, Ben worked at the top cardiothoracic hospitals including University College hospital, the Brompton and Guy's hospitals, training under the auspices of the cardiac surgeon Russell Brock, who had a significant influence on his work.

In 1958 he was appointed the first consultant cardiothoracic surgeon for Papworth and Addenbrooke's hospitals. During the subsequent 26 years, he devoted his professional life to developing and establishing a world-class centre for cardiothoracic surgery. In addition, from 1977 to 1984, he was an associate lecturer in the Cambridge University clinical school, where he taught anatomy.

In 1960, Ben became one of the first in the UK to use the heart–lung machine, which kept the body's vital organs functioning while surgery took place and is now a standard piece of equipment. Two years earlier, in preparation, he and his team performed trials by experimenting on dogs and pigs at the School of Veterinary Medicine in Cambridge. At first they worked in the gardener's hut and later in the postmortem room. These places were freezing cold in winter and it was necessary to wear a full skiing outfit beneath one's surgical gown.

In 1969, Ben and Roy Calne together decided to investigate the possibility of cardiac transplantation. They attempted auto and homo transplantation on animals in the laboratory. In auto transplantation, the heart is taken out and replaced in the same animal; in homo (or allo) transplantation, a heart is placed in another of the same species. There were no long-term survivors, the longest being five hours, and these efforts then had to be abandoned due to lack of funding. It was not until 1979 that Terence English successfully performed the first clinical cardiac transplant – on a person – at Papworth.

Ben's surgical career spanned the entire development of cardiac surgery, and throughout he maintained an active practice in thoracic surgery. He was an ardent supporter of the NHS and strived to maintain the highest possible standards for his patients. He introduced the concept of co-operation rather than competition in the running of the surgical unit. He believed that this policy of good team-work involving every discipline contributed to the success of the cardiothoracic unit. A father figure at Papworth, he was known for his wise counsel and forthright attitude; I met him in 1981, when I went there as a consultant.

He was awarded a Hunterian professorship by the Royal College of Surgeons in 1956 (cardiac arrest and resuscitation), and was given the Royal College of Surgeons' Jacksonian prize in 1957 (pathology and treatment of aneurysms). He was president of the Thoracic Society in 1980 and editor of *Thorax* from 1978 to 1983. Ben, Peter James and other cardiothoracic surgeons in 1959 founded Pete's club, the constitution of which declared that the scientific business should be the discussion of mistakes and errors of judgment; no member was allowed to report a case that reflected credit on himself. It expanded nationally and internationally into Europe and finally the US. It was disbanded in 1989, but was a forerunner of the clinical governance and audit that are standard today; cardiac surgery in particular is now at the vanguard of open scrutiny.

Ben was born in Dublin, the fourth child and first son of Jewish immigrant parents, Hershel and Rebecca. The family moved to Hampstead, north London, where his father worked as a tailor. After primary education, he won a place at St Marylebone grammar school. He gained an open scholarship to read medicine at University College London, where he qualified in 1942. During his student days, having abandoned all Jewish ritual and beliefs, he marched in support of Spanish antifascists and was committed to socialist ideals for his entire life. In 1942, he was conscripted into the Royal Army Medical Corps, became an acting major, and landed in Normandy three days after D-Day, eventually seeing service in France, Belgium, the Netherlands and Germany. He was mentioned twice in dispatches for valour and courage.

After retirement he was able to devote more of his time to his many hobbies. At a violin-making class in Cambridge he made two violins, a cello and finally a viola, thus completing his string quartet. He had a wonderful sense of humour, was a brilliant conversationalist and entertainer and successfully turned his hand to painting and gardening.

The Heart–Lung Machine Department

In January 1959 Dr Claude Lum arrived at Papworth. He had been a director of the sanatorium at Nayland in Suffolk, which had been closed because of the falling incidence of tuberculosis. Dr Lum took charge of the extracorporeal part of the heart–lung machine programme and operated the pump for the early cases. As the perfusion service developed, Dr Lum was joined by the two chest physicians, Dr E.M. Cheffins and Dr Martin Greenberg. The cleaning and preparation of the Melrose oxygenator – a time-consuming and demanding chore – was in the expert hands of Charles Hubbard, the theatre superintendent.

The first member of the staff to devote his whole time to the heart–lung machine was Roy Gill, who was appointed as a technician in 1967. He was sent to the Brompton Hospital in 1968 for training, and with the experience he gained there he introduced the then new oxygenator to the Papworth unit. Meanwhile Dr Lum was developing the department of Respiratory Physiology and so his involvement in the heart–lung machine became progressively less.

In 1969 Dr Don Bethune was appointed as consultant anaesthetist with an interest in cardiopulmonary bypass (CPB), a far-sighted step. However, in 1971 the sudden death of Dr Greenberg deprived the Heart–Lung Department of both chest physicians, because Cheffins then had to cope with a doubled workload in the Chest Department. Dr Bethune and Roy Gill were then left to carry on the service on their own.

During the subsequent twelve years the Department grew with the increase in clinical work, and engaged in a wide range of research activities related to cardiopulmonary bypass.

By then there were five trained technicians and one trainee providing for over 450 open-heart cases per annum. Their work encompassed many other activities including physiological monitoring in the theatre and at the bedside, provision of an intra-aortic balloon counterpulsation service, running the blood gas laboratory in the operating theatre and taking part in the cardiac transplant programme.

As in most units at this time, cardiac surgery was a risky business, with the initial operative mortality of the order of 40 per cent. Respiratory complications causing bleeding in the lungs and infection were the commonest. Most patients required prolonged ventilation and many had to have a tracheostomy. Another major problem was heart failure, which resulted from inadequate protection of the heart muscle when the heart was disconnected from the circulation so that heart surgery could be performed on a still, non-beating heart during the period of aortic clamping.

The doctors and surgeons were well aware of the problem and tried every method including ischaemia, coronary perfusion with normothermic blood and with blood at temperatures down to 10°C, iced slush in the pericardium and continuous pericardial cooling, but none of these appeared to provide the answer. There are various ways of protecting the heart, and heart surgery is now much safer.

In 1963, because of the shortage of nurses, a post-registration course was started. This was long before the Joint Board of Clinical Nursing had come into effect. By some extensive and inevitably expensive advertising, the hospital was able to attract an extra ten qualified nurses, which made it possible to keep the work going. They managed to perform about 40 open-heart cases a year until 1970, when they had to stop completely because the nursing shortage had become dangerous. However, in 1971 and

1972 the number of open-heart cases reached 100 per year, and by this time the mortality rate had fallen in a straight line to about 10 per cent. At that time there were two full-time anaesthetists with appropriate supporting staff.

During the 1960s and early 70s the operation lists were very heavy. Operations started at 8.00am and carried on to 8.00pm without stopping for lunch. In this way they were able to perform about 700 major procedures per annum on both heart and lungs.

However, life was not all work. At lunchtime on the days when they did not operate, the surgeons and consultants would retire to the first-floor dining room in Papworth Hall, where, surrounded by Saumarez portraits and a Guido Reni, they were served an excellent three-course lunch. Following this they would either move to the billiard room next door for a frame of snooker or, in the winter, they might take their guns to the woods behind the hospital to find a pheasant for Sunday lunch. In the spring a mass of primroses, violets, cowslips and bluebells in the woods spread a dappled pattern of blue and yellow, a delightful sight on which to rest the eyes in a pause during a difficult operation.

There was a friendly atmosphere in Papworth Hospital too, which could not be reproduced in a larger hospital. For example, the charge nurse in the operating theatre was also the COHSE shop steward. On one occasion they were due to take part in a strike. The nurse came to see Milstein and said: 'Look sir, we are supposed to be going on strike but I don't want to cause any trouble. Do you think you could make sure the operating stops at eight o'clock?'

This explains the cultural ethos that has made Papworth Hospital so special.

These were the operations at Papworth Hospital from 1958 to 1964:

	1958	1959	1962	1964
TB	47	21	14	5
Other lung	108	57	106	63
Heart operations				
Oesophagus	25	21	60	49
Mitral valvotomy	15	18	25	10
PDA	5	10	9	4
ASD	6	6	19	13
VSD Fallot	–	–	9	8
Aortic aneurysm	1	4	9	2
Other operations				
Peripheral vascular	4	23	59	40

As we have seen, when Hugh Fleming arrived at Papworth Hospital in October 1959, Chris Parish and Ben Milstein, two surgeons there, had been doing a small amount of closed cardiac surgery and were doing animal work at the Veterinary School using the heart–lung machine on pigs, and later, dogs. They were assisted by the chest physicians, Martin Greenberg, Michael Cheffins and Claude Lum.

There were no other cardiac clinics in East Anglia, but gradually clinics were established in King's Lynn, Wisbech, Doddington, Peterborough, Stamford, Ipswich, Newmarket and Saffron Walden. In King's Lynn, the only room available was in the dental clinic and Hugh Fleming got used to examining patients who were sitting in a dental chair.

Fleming noted that:

In the early days when I suggested admission to Papworth patients' faces frequently fell in dismay. It turned out that Papworth had the stigma of either tuberculosis or cancer of the lung. This was difficult to shake off and initially patients would not always believe my reassurance that they had neither of these diseases. However, it did not take long for the word to spread around that the Cardiac Unit was a Good Place and for the rest of my time at Papworth I found it very difficult to admit patients to other newer and bigger hospitals – they all wanted to return to Papworth. They knew Papworth, they liked the friendly atmosphere, they trusted the place and they were very reluctant to enter any other hospital. This feeling frequently persisted even after they had survived another hospital admission where the surroundings were certainly slicker and more modern.

When the patients began to be referred, it was quite evident that we were dealing with a very backward area. First of all the phlegmatic patients of the Fens would put up with incredible disability before they consulted a doctor. Secondly, many of the doctors were reluctant to refer them, not being aware of what modern treatment could offer. The resulting variety of severe cardiac pathology was quite extraordinary and medical staff coming to us from London teaching hospitals were amazed at this. Right from the beginning we dealt with children as well as adults. In those days there were no paediatric cardiologists in the country so we dealt with neonates onwards. I saw many neonatal cases in the Mill Road Maternity Hospital and older children on the children's ward. Children also formed a large proportion of the out-patients, frequently referred from the school medical service because of murmurs. The authoritative dismissal of many of these as being innocent was a most important function.

Background to cardiology at Papworth

It is now a suitable time to explain why cardiology should have come to a place like Papworth. This was part of a pattern that, after the war, was repeated all over the country and, indeed, in many other parts of the world.

In the 1950s pulmonary tuberculosis remained a major health problem and an organisation of sanatoria, chest hospitals and chest clinics had been developed to cope with it. With the advent of surgical treatment for tuberculosis, operating theatres and supporting hospital facilities had been added, and the speciality of thoracic surgery grew. This, helped by the arrival of antibacterial drugs, was so successful that within a few years the problem began to be controlled. This left the surgical units and their experienced staff of surgeons, anaesthetists, nurses and technicians with under-employed resources. Therefore it was natural that, as cardiac surgery was developed by the same teams, it should do so in the same sanatoria. In the post-war years all resources were in short supply and much development was opportunistic rather than deliberately planned.

Specialist cardiology developed largely in response to the surgical need for accurate diagnosis and assessment before operation, so it grew alongside surgery. Cardiology soon became a complete speciality and its demands were such that there was little time left to its practitioners for general medical work. The result was that much of the early development of cardiology, outside the London teaching hospitals, occurred in chest hospitals and sanatoria and remained there for some time.

We should look at the heart itself and see why it can become necessary for it to have treatment. Professor John Wallwork and Rob Stepney wrote a book, *Heart Disease*, which was published in 1987. In it they wrote:

Though not much larger than a clenched fist, the heart's daily 100,000 beats circulate almost 2,000 gallons of blood. In a year, this extraordinary pump beats non-stop between 30 and 40 million times – in a lifetime, two and a half billion times. In its tirelessness and reliability, the heart is an example of supreme biological engineering. But, as with any engine, it relies on its components. The heart has chambers that collect and distribute blood, valves that regulate its flow, muscle that provides power, an electrical system to control the timing of the whole process and piping that supplies the heart muscle itself with blood, and so with the oxygen and nutrients it needs for fuel.

Any or all of these components may fail: chambers may have holes, valves may leak, muscle may become flabby and electrical circuits are liable to disconnections and short-circuits. Each problem gives rise to a different form of heart disease. But the most common difficulty is with the heart's own fuel supply. It arises because the vessels serving the heart muscle – the coronary arteries – become lined with fatty deposits which restrict and ultimately block the flow of blood. Without sufficient blood, there is too little oxygen and food for the heart tissues. It is this that leads to the pain of angina, and the death of heart muscle in a heart attack that can fatally cripple the heart's ability to function. Around eight out of ten patients with cardiac problems have disease of the coronary arteries.

There are many different heart problems: birth defects, valve disease – narrowing and leakage, coronary artery disease – 'hardening of the arteries', congenital heart disease, problems with heart muscle, abnormal heart rates and rhythms, breathlessness, pain, palpitations, fainting, swelling, pulse rate and blood pressure. Wallwork and Stepney went on to outline all the possible heart defects and how they could be treated. (It was a long time since Theodore Billroth, the Prussian-born Austrian, acknowledged as the founding father of abdominal surgery, had said in 1883: 'The surgeon who should attempt to suture a wound of the heart would lose all the respect of his colleagues', and since Sir James Paget had said in 1896: 'Surgery of the heart has probably reached the limits set by nature to all surgery: no new method and no discovery can overcome the natural difficulties that attend a wound of the heart.')

Wallwork and Stepney concluded with a chapter entitled 'The Future', in which they wrote:

Heart attacks are clearly the most important problem in heart disease. Roughly 50 per cent of the quarter million that occur in Britain each year are fatal. So, if we are really to make an impact on death and disability, it must be done by improving our treatment of this condition. Whatever the long-term factors that increase risk, it is now generally agreed that the immediate cause of a heart attack is the formation of a clot – called a thrombus – that blocks a coronary artery. One hope is that we will be able to find an easily administered and safe drug that dissolves that clot and so restores the flow of blood. If this is done, heart muscle can be prevented from dying.

Cardiac catheterisation and the X-ray Department

In the 1950s the X-ray Department was in the Surgical Unit, which was a free-standing block across a small road and a courtyard from the Cardiac Unit. A flight of steps led up to the entrance. It was many years before the connecting bridge between the two blocks was built.

The X-ray Department was the bottleneck that controlled all the hospital work for very many years and it was rigidly run by Dr Duncan Gregg, who was appointed consultant radiologist at Addenbrooke's and Papworth in 1954. Apparently, he did not welcome the advent of cardiology and put many obstacles in the path of the development work. Patiently dealing with these in an effort to achieve a sufficient number of cardiac catheterisations was

exhausting and time-consuming. A dedicated cardiac catheter laboratory was desperately needed, but was not made
available for many years. More than once, detailed plans
for this laboratory were drawn up but they were not implemented. Perhaps there should be a degree of sympathy for
Dr Gregg's position. The fact was that he had established
and equipped an excellent department for his angiography
and no planning had been made for the needs of cardiology,
which suddenly put an unwelcome burden on his resources.
As already mentioned, the stresses of work in those pioneering days were ever-present in the hospital, and away
from it Duncan Gregg could apparently be very charming.

The X-ray Department in the Surgical Unit consisted
of a single room into which had to be fitted all the work
– routine chest X-rays, barium studies, tomography, angio-
grams and cardiac catheterisation. To arrange all this was a
major problem and inevitably led to one team being played
off against another. Gregg was particularly interested in
peripheral vascular disease and this would always be given
priority, in spite of the urgent demands of cardiac patients.
When eventually in 1966 a second small room across the
corridor was handed over to the X-ray Department there
was considerably less pressure, but the problems remained.

Dr Gregg, in the interests of angiography, had very good
equipment for the time – infinitely better than that at the
Brompton. There was a Philips image intensifier with a
5-inch screen for fluoroscopy for catheterisation, and a
Schönander biplane cut film changer for angiography.

Eventually they managed to work things up to a fairly
regular three catheters a week, but Dr Ron Gold, a senior

registrar, recalled the enormous weekly tussles that he had to endure to achieve this. Gregg insisted on personally being present every second that the footswitch controlling the screening was depressed. As he might leave the room while blood sampling and exercise were being undertaken, this often meant a fairly fraught and prolonged procedure. There was just one Sanborn electromanometer. Cardiac catheters were relatively primitive, really just simple tubes. A small bend could be made on the end and, by virtue of this, it was possible to drive, manipulate and rotate them through the right side of the heart. This was a skilful procedure and had to be carried out with great care. It must be remembered that defibrillators and pacemakers had not yet been developed and any serious arrhythmia would have meant death on the catheter table. Happily there were no such cases, though, not surprisingly, there were some nasty frights.

Even external cardiac massage was not yet in use, and in the event of resuscitation being necessary, open chest message would have to be attempted. A thoracotomy kit was part of the back-up equipment for cardiac investigation and always to hand. Catheters had to be kept meticulously clean as they were re-sterilised and re-used. As already mentioned, initially investigations were confined to right heart catheters and left ventricular puncture. The Seldinger technique (used for angiography, insertion of chest drains and central venous catheters, insertion of PEG tubes using the push technique, insertion of the leads for an artificial pacemaker or implantable cardioverter-defibrillator, and numerous other interventional medical procedures) was soon introduced by Dr Gregg, and Dr Martin Greenberg was a keen and skilful proponent of the Radner procedure – i.e. retrosternal insertion of a needle going down through the aorta to the pulmonary artery and the left atrium, measuring pressures on the way. Ben Milstein was also involved in starting this procedure.

Precision of diagnosis was of absolutely fundamental importance. Skilled though the surgeons were, they had few facilities to cope with the unexpected. It was imperative to know that an atrial septal defect was a simple defect rather than a complicated one involving other structures in the heart, and that mitral stenosis in adults was pure without any significant leakage. Failure to achieve this accuracy of diagnosis would mean either an unnecessary operation or even a fatal outcome.

Patients had to be manually transported from the Cardiac Unit to the catheter room and back. This consisted of lifting them on to a canvas stretcher, placing it on a trolley, pushing it up the hill to the Surgical Unit, lifting the stretcher off the trolley to carry it up the steps, and putting it back on the trolley to wheel into the X-ray Department – with the reverse journey after the procedure. This had to be carried out in all weathers, which in those days seemed to include a lot of snow. There was a special canvas cover to keep the weather off – this was not unlike those that were used for taking bodies to the morgue, but it was effective. There were no porters, so it was a matter of gathering what volunteers one could, and these were never lacking to form a team. A nurse who knew the patient always went to the catheter room to act as 'patient's friend' throughout the procedure. All this was carried out with willing, good humour and happily without mortality. Later, in bad weather, patients made the short journey by a primitive ambulance, which was also used for general transport purposes about the hospital site.

In 1964 a bridge was eventually built between the Cardiac Unit and the Surgical Unit so that patients could be wheeled over under cover and on one level. This made an enormous difference and greatly improved safety.

All the chest X-rays for the Cardiac Unit were carried out in the Bernhard Baron Hospital, and much time was spent transferring patients from the Cardiac Unit, coping with the slow and unreliable lift, pushing them in wheelchairs down the very rough road or getting them in and out of the above-mentioned ambulance. Portable films could be done on the ward but they were of unsatisfactory quality.

Dr G.I. Verney (Bob) was appointed senior registrar in radiology in 1964, having come from Newcastle and Shotley Bridge. He was appointed consultant in 1965 and remained in post until he retired in 1992. He remembers that a large number of children with congenital heart disease were catheterised, and when there were equipment problems at Papworth the whole team would have to move to the old Addenbrooke's site in Cambridge, where the barium room was used. Apparently, Verney's arrival, with his skills and placid temperament, was very welcome.

There was considerable anxiety over the catheterising of very small and sick cyanosed babies, and there was much gratitude that the Mayo Clinic in the USA published a paper on Howell–Jolly bodies in the peripheral blood. These are associated with asplenia (absence of normal spleen function), which goes with impossibly complicated congenital cardiac defects. The presence of these bodies indicated that detailed investigation would be a waste of time as no corrective surgery would be possible in those days. There was also gratitude to the haematologist for providing an emergency service and relief when the hospital could with a clear conscience withdraw from active investigation in such cases.

Edmond Groves was the superintendent radiographer until he retired in 1965. Happily, a room in the present department bears his name. He had a difficult task dealing with Duncan Gregg. Groves was a shy gentleman who was a meticulous radiographer and who also, given time, produced excellent slides from X-rays. He remained unmarried and lived in the small lodge at the south side of the entrance of the Hall drive. His story was an interesting one. He had been a medical student at Sidney Sussex College, Cambridge, when he developed pulmonary tuberculosis. He had needed a great deal of treatment over the years and was never able to return to practise medicine.

In 1967 the group was joined by Dr D.W. Evans, when the cardiology load had grown too great for Dr Fleming to handle. Dr Evans' particular expertise was cardiac pacemaking. At first this involved a surgical operation, either a small one to expose a vein, or a thoracotomy to expose the heart. For a period this activity became very time-consuming, but fortunately the cardiologists discovered the means of making and closing an incision themselves. They were soon coping successfully with almost all cardiac pacing and rarely needed to call for surgical help.

One cardiologist who had enormous influence at Papworth was Hugh Fleming. As we have seen, in 1959, when he started at Papworth, he was the first cardiologist to be appointed in East Anglia. For seven years he worked single-handed; a second cardiologist was appointed in 1966 and it was not until 1977 that they were joined by a third colleague.

The cardiology registrars that Fleming trained are now consultants throughout the world. He was a gifted, hard-working and caring teacher, and did original research that enabled the diagnosis of sarcoid heart disease, which hitherto was recognised only post-mortem. He did it all having overcome tuberculosis himself and, in the early days, considerable discouragement.

Born in New Zealand, Fleming came to the UK and worked at the Brompton Hospital in London under Guy Scadding and Paul Wood, two of the founders of British cardiology, and, significantly, a young cardiothoracic surgeon, Ben Milstein.

Cardiology was in its early stages at the Brompton and was barely tolerated. Fleming had to do cardiac catheterisation at 8.00am in the X-ray Department before the department opened for normal business at 9.00am, and often the films were sabotaged by the radiographer. He recalled that the consultants wore morning suits, many were prima donnas, and most arrived at the hospital in Rolls-Royces driven by their chauffeur, to be met on the steps by a fawning matron and their juniors. Fleming often assisted Lord Brock in the operating theatre, silently and stoically tolerating the great man's verbal abuse. Towards the end of this time Ben Milstein was appointed as heart surgeon at Papworth and Fleming often travelled, unpaid and in his own time, to Cambridge, to perform and teach cardiac catheterisation.

Fleming moved back to Australia but, in 1958, he received a telephone call enquiring if he would be interested in setting up cardiology at Papworth Hospital. Milstein set him up, but the early days were not easy.

The Chairman of the Addenbrooke's medical council told Fleming: 'I understand there is no need of a cardiologist in East Anglia, but I expect you will find something to do.' The Regius Professor of Medicine, Joe Mitchell, broke down in tears, saying he did not know why Fleming had come there and that Cambridge was an awful place which had treated him abysmally.

Fleming built up the department from scratch, providing diagnostic services for the heart surgeons, working single-handed for many years, training generations of heart specialists, and earning their love and loyalty. It was a slow start. GPs in the region sent him patients – he saw 800 new patients in his first year and more thereafter – but Cambridge physicians cold-shouldered him and he had no beds for admitting patients. They were, however, happy for him to look after their in-patients when they took a day off to go shooting together.

He had to fight to get accommodation for a weekly clinic at Addenbrooke's. His department suffered from the lack of co-operation between the Regional Hospital Board and that of the Cambridge hospitals and from the internecine feuds of the Cambridge consultants. Fleming travelled all over East Anglia in his Baby Austin, seeing patients in a dozen small towns. Most were reluctant to be admitted to Papworth and had to be reassured that they had neither TB nor cancer, both of which were considered shameful. The hospital in Norwich, which had cardiac ambitions of its own, refused for some years to refer patients to him, and sent them to London instead.

Fleming was ahead of his time in many of the things he did: when a child had to be admitted, he would put them in a two-bedded room with one of their parents, long before this was established practice. He made a practice of labelling patients' medicines, which was considered taboo in those days. He abolished the undignified practice of making patients undress before a consultation, even though this often made the consultation last considerably longer, especially with the elderly. In the 1960s he introduced the pacemaking service.

He supported the surgical service. He ran postgraduate courses for hospital doctors, which resulted in referrals from outside the area, including north London. He overcame the nursing shortage by running post-qualification courses for nurses. He sidestepped committees because, he said, 'they started at 2.00pm and went on through the afternoon at a leisurely pace'. In 1961 he was offered the chair of cardiology in Sydney and turned it down.

Fleming's professional isolation among the Cambridge physicians came to a dramatic end when one of them was ill and needed his services. He gradually became cardiologist to 100 doctors with heart disease in the region. In the early days, the evidence connecting smoking with heart disease was unknown and many doctors and their patients were heavy smokers.

Fleming did some private work. There was a certain amount of hostility to private in-patients at Papworth, who got the same food as NHS patients but on china plates; however, they were served last so that their food arrived cold. All patients, whether NHS or private, were put in the same cramped, shabby rooms, which were so small that a patient needing resuscitation had to be dragged into the corridor. Fleming did private consultations at home. This being Cambridge, many patients arrived on bicycles, and Fleming was probably the only consultant cardiologist in the UK with a patients' bicycle rack outside his house.

Many of the Fenland patients had rustic standards of cleanliness – they would wash their face to visit the doctor but did not expect to have to remove their shoes, and 'often their feet were beyond description'.

Fleming wrote a detailed annual report and submitted it to the Regional Medical Officer, but regrettably these were all destroyed. However, Fleming kept a copy of his report from January 1962:

Dr J.B. Ewen
Senior Administrative Medical Officer
East Anglian Regional Hospital Board
117 Chesterton Road
Cambridge

Dear Dr Ewen,
I thought you would be interested to have some basic figures of the volume of work in the Cardiac Unit at the end of its second complete calendar year in operation.

The volume of work has steadily increased and there is no sign of this trend diminishing. The pattern of work has not changed since I last reported to you. With a few very notable exceptions I am not referred a great number of cases by general physicians. Most of the patients tend to come direct from their general practitioner.

In the calendar year of 1961 I personally saw 880 new patients in the region. This compares with the figure of 839 for the calendar year of 1960. Most of the top floor of the Princess Hospital at Papworth is now available for cardiac patients and we usually run at an occupied bed suite of something over twenty. This does not, of course, include the cardiac patients who will be in surgical beds at the same time. In 1961 we admitted 324 patients to the Cardiac Unit. This is in contrast to 206 patients for the year 1960.

In 1961 we carried out 112 cardiac catheterisations. This number is limited by the number of times a week that Dr Gregg can allow us into his department for catheterisation. It has also been limited by the need for the cardiac team to be involved with heart–lung machine surgery. We now have two technicians sufficiently well trained so that we are able to carry out cardiac catheterisation at the same time as a pump operation is taking place upstairs. Eighty-two cardiac operations have been carried out and many of these have required pressure monitoring by the cardiac team. Twenty-two angiocardiograms have been carried out and this again requires co-operation between the cardiac and the radiological teams. Six hundred and eight electrocardiograms have been carried out.

As you know, I feel that if a unit such as mine is to

justify itself it must carry out work of the highest standard. I do feel that in the past year we have satisfactorily consolidated ourselves in this respect. Dr Gold and Dr Izukawa are both now well trained and very reliable. I feel that the continued standard of the Unit depends to a considerable extent on being able to replace these young men by others of similar calibre.

I am sure that the above figures emphasise the need for increased laboratory space for the Unit and particularly for a projected cardiac catheterisation room so that we can carry out many more procedures independent of the existing facilities in the X-ray Department.

With kind regards.

Yours sincerely,

H.A. Fleming
Consultant Cardiologist

Fleming published about 70 research papers, mainly on infectious endocarditis and sarcoid heart disease, and an account of the early years, *Papworth Cardiac Unit 1957–1967* (1966). He retired completely in 1988, aged 65, commenting: 'You can't be a part-time cardiologist in the NHS.'

Chris Flower joined the team as a radiologist in 1973. He remembers that neither Ben Milstein nor Chris Parish felt the need to use radiologists. Milstein had worked under Russell, later Lord Brock, who certainly did not see the need for them. (Radiology is a medical term for the use of imaging to diagnose and treat disease.)

Nevertheless, Flower persisted in his development of radiology and the next generation of surgeons at Papworth, including Terence English, John Wallwork and Francis Wells, welcomed his advice. There would be quite heated discussions about the best treatment for a patient and often Flower would say that, in his opinion, surgery was not necessary. However, his views were always treated with respect and he felt that the surgeons were happy to have the 'road-map' that radiologists provided.

Furthermore, Flower pushed out the boundaries of radiology, pioneering new techniques. He ensured that Papworth was at the forefront of new imaging possibilities, some of which he and his colleagues had developed. Among their developments were percutaneous techniques, such as lung biopsy and pleural drainage. He also recognised the importance of cross-sectional imaging in the investigation and management of malignant and diffuse lung disease, and collaborated with others such as Peter Stovin and John Stark, a chest physician, in the introduction of new techniques such as flexible bronchoscopy so that they were accepted quickly.

Peter Stovin, a consultant histopathologist, helped to determine an international standard for heart and lung biopsies. He went to Papworth Hospital as a consultant histopathologist from the London Hospital in autumn 1960. At that time his work was mostly related to the surgical lung specimens with only occasional cardiac autopsies. However, in 1979 everything changed with the start of heart transplantation.

In 1979 Stovin went to Stanford University in California for a short course on heart transplant pathology, led by

Dr Margaret Billingham. He realised that he was handling unique material and he helped other cardiac research workers; this involved being present at the transplant operation. Together with David Spiegelhalter in 1983 he determined a new system for monitoring biopsy specimens in transplant patients which became the recommended standard of the International Society for Heart and Lung Transplantation (ISHLT). He wrote the chapter on heart pathology in R.Y. Calne's *Transplantation Immunology: clinical and experimental* (1984) and in John Wallwork's *Heart and Heart–Lung Transplantation* (1989).

In evidence to the Redfern Inquiry (2008) into the retention of surgical and autopsy material by hospitals, Dr Stovin pointed out that retention was necessary as one in ten transplant patients had been keen to see their own removed organ and that he fully expected some relatives would want burial or cremation to include the original diseased organ. Dr Stovin retired in 1986.

In 1981, John Stark had been joined by the consultant respiratory physician, Tim Higenbottam, who developed lung biopsies in transplant patients with John Scott and Susan Stewart. They doubled the survival rates of lung transplant patients and co-discovered three medical treatments for pulmonary hypertension.

Higenbottam introduced transbronchial lung biopsies with the support of pathology colleagues, including Peter Stovin, to monitor infection and rejection in lung transplant patients. As we shall see later, with colleagues John Wallwork and Francis Wells, Professor Higenbottam began the revolution of medical care of patients with pulmonary arterial hypertension (PAH) with the discovery that intravenous prostacyclin increased survival. He then co-discovered two further treatments of PAH, inhaled nitric oxide for neonates and oral sildenafil. In the UK some 3,000 patients with PAH now survive on medical care alone, reducing the need for lung transplant surgery.

After leaving Papworth Hospital in 1995 to become Professor of Medicine in Sheffield, Higenbottam led the collaboration of the UK PAH centres, including Papworth, to establish the National Network of Pulmonary Hypertension clinics in 2001. These have provided a global standard for the care of patients and facilitated advances in scientific knowledge of PAH.

This multi-disciplinary approach provided the impetus for improved patient care and the opportunity for collaborative research, especially in focal and diffuse lung disease, thromboembolic disease and lung transplantation.

Chapter 3

HEART TRANSPLANTS

Cardiac transplantation
The first heart transplant
'Getting a kick out of life'

Cardiac transplantation

In October 1969 Professor R.Y. Calne and Ben Milstein got together and decided to investigate the possibilities of cardiac transplantation. These experiments were carried out at the Department of Surgery in Douglas House in Cambridge and in the Veterinary School. The technique which was used on both pigs and dogs was essentially the same as was used in human cardiac transplantation.

Calne and Milstein attempted both auto- and homo-transplantation but had no long-term survivors, the longest being about five hours, as we have seen. The reason for this was bleeding from the atrial anastomosis. The suture material available at the time made much larger stitch holes than could be obtained by using polypropylene, which made the control of bleeding in a thin atrium so simple years later. They abandoned the technique after some months of experimentation when the money ran out. However, they had made one great discovery, or rather rediscovery.

On one occasion when Milstein used diathermy to incise the skin of a pig which had been doused too liberally with an alcoholic antiseptic, there was a flash, a crack and the air was filled with a strong smell of crackling. Thus they discovered a simple technique for achieving what, according to Charles Lamb, had required in China the burning down of an entire house – namely, the production of roast pork.

At the end of 1972 Christopher Parish became Postgraduate Dean and had virtually given up clinical activities. Milstein was then joined by Terence English. Milstein said later:

One thing I had determined very firmly having seen pairs of surgeons working elsewhere, was that we would co-operate and not compete. With this in mind, I arranged that the beds and waiting lists were common. We carried out ward rounds together and quite often operated on one another's patients. This necessitated a considerable sacrifice on my part since it involved yielding to a large extent the position of senior surgeon to which I had just succeeded. However, this policy was very effective and I am sure contributed greatly to the success of the Cardiothoracic Unit at that time. It is difficult for such a policy to succeed when more than two individuals are involved and even then incompatible personalities may render this kind of partnership quite unrealistic.

The first heart transplant

The 1960s was an important decade in the development of treatments to tackle the various heart and lung ailments.

The major breakthrough was the introduction of the heart–lung machine. This was the key to open-heart surgery. It meant the surgeon could divert the blood returning to the heart into the machine, which oxygenated the blood before pumping it back into the aorta, thereby bypassing both the heart and the lungs. This meant the heart could be stopped or cooled, giving access to make repairs in a bloodless environment.

Further progress was made in the 1970s and in 1977 the first angioplasty was performed. This procedure, which involves inserting a balloon into the blocked or narrowed artery and then inflating it, is now carried out more than 20,000 times a year in the UK alone.

The world's first heart transplant was carried out at Groote Schuur Hospital in South Africa on 3 December 1967. The surgical team was led by Professor Christiaan Barnard.

The operation captured the imagination of the whole world and shot Barnard to international fame, though it is interesting to note that others who were also deeply engaged in heart surgery were not as impressed.

Although this is a book about Papworth Hospital, a surgeon who must be mentioned is Norman Shumway, because of his pioneering work in the development of heart transplants.

He performed the first successful human heart transplant in the USA at Stanford in 1968. In spite of controversy over legal and economic issues, particularly of what constitutes brain death among potential donors, Shumway and his colleagues persisted. Philip Pizzo, Dean of Stanford School of Medicine, called Shumway 'one of the 20th century's true pioneers in cardiac surgery. He developed one of the world's most distinguished departments of cardiothoracic surgery at Stanford, trained leaders who now guide this field throughout the world and created a record of accomplishment that few will ever rival. His impact will be long-lived and his name long-remembered.'

By the time Shumway died at the age of 83 in 2007 nearly 60,000 patients in the USA had lived longer lives because of new hearts, and at Stanford alone 1,240 patients had received new hearts. Thanks to his close relationship with John Wallwork, Shumway did come to Papworth to work for six months following his retirement.

Terence, now Sir Terence, English said later, after he had visited Stanford University in 1972:

I was interested to see patients who were doing well after heart transplantation and I became inspired by the enthusiasm for the future of the heart surgeons including Dr Shumway. Although Barnard had done the first heart transplant, Shumway and his colleague, Richard Lower, had done nearly all the early important experimental work, refining the surgical technique and investigating the phenomenon of rejection after transplantation and how this might be modified. So their disappointment was great when Barnard achieved primacy by doing the first case. I had spent a week in 1963 observing Barnard's work in Cape Town and had come away unimpressed by his technical skills and behaviour in the operating theatre, although I had to recognise his good results which derived from an obsessive attention to detail.

He continued:

Like many others, I was surprised to hear of his first two transplants on 3 December 1967 and 2 January 1968. Shumway followed with his first on 6 January and soon cardiac surgeons all over the world were attempting to transplant hearts, usually with poor results. Indeed, of the 166 patients who received hearts during 1968, 1969 and 1970 only just over half lived for more than a month and

11 per cent more than two years. Amongst these were three patients transplanted by my mentor Donald Ross, but in keeping with results elsewhere in the world they only survived for short periods (45, 2 and 107 days). So in January 1973, the Chief Medical Officer for Health, Sir George Godber, declared what amounted to a moratorium on further attempts at heart transplantation in Britain.

Nevertheless, research continued and on his return to Papworth, English discussed with Ben Milstein the idea of Papworth being the UK centre where heart transplantation research should be pursued. Milstein did not want to be personally involved in the actual transplant operations but was very supportive.

Meanwhile Roy, now Sir Roy, Calne had made great progress in kidney and liver transplantation as well as transplantation of pig hearts, working at Addenbrooke's Hospital in Cambridge. English approached Calne, who responded enthusiastically. The first formal meeting between them took place in October 1973. Those at the meeting included David Evans, the neurologist with whom Calne worked, Ben Milstein and the two Papworth consultant cardiologists, Hugh Fleming and David Wainwright Evans. According to English, 'it was clear from the start that the Cardiologists did not want to be involved. Hugh Fleming was neutral in his stance whereas David Evans expressed strong opposition on both clinical and religious grounds and subsequently, during all the years that followed, remained highly critical of the work even to the extent of publicly accusing me of removing hearts from people who were still alive.'

Nevertheless, at that meeting it was agreed that they would work towards establishing heart transplantation in Cambridge, primarily at Addenbrooke's. In autumn 1974, after training the necessary ICU (intensive care unit) and theatre staff, a series of open-heart operations was carried out at Addenbrooke's with Professor Calne and his senior registrar assisting English and anaesthetists and heart–lung technicians from Papworth.

Further progress was made, but in early 1976 events caused concern to English. He said later:

The experimental work went well and we began to get more regular survivors after transplanting hearts into pigs. And then in March 1976, the Professor of Medicine, Ivor Mills, referred us a patient for consideration of transplantation. I was due to leave for a cardiology meeting in Hong Kong in a few days but I first made a careful assessment of the patient who was 59 years old and had an advanced cardiomyopathy. He was cachectic due to long-standing heart failure with incipient gangrene of his toes and I considered him too old and too sick to be suitable for transplantation. I asked Hugh Fleming to see the patient and he concurred with my decision. I then wrote to Roy Calne with a copy to Ivor Mills, providing them with a full report of my assessment, and left for Hong Kong. On my return a fortnight later I was amazed to learn that during my absence Roy Calne had decided to proceed with a transplant if a donor heart could be found.

In the event this was not possible and the patient died just one week after I had seen him. However, the reaction to Roy's decision at Addenbrooke's was intense and we were forcefully reminded of our agreement to seek approval from the Medical Committee before embarking on clinical cardiac transplantation at Addenbrooke's. This made me recognise that the difficulties associated with doing the work at Addenbrooke's were substantial and the incident also caused me to question Roy Calne's judgement. And so it was that I began to believe that the best place for the programme to be developed was at Papworth Hospital. Furthermore, as a cardiac surgical procedure it seemed logical that the operation should be done by cardiac surgeons, with anaesthetists and nursing staff familiar with dealing with very sick cardiac patients on a daily basis and with dedicated theatre and intensive care facilities on site. I also considered the general ambience of Papworth more suitable for potentially long-stay transplant patients and their families than that of Addenbrooke's.

At a meeting after my return from Hong Kong I expressed some of these views to Roy but no agreement was reached as to the best way forward. In April we were asked to meet with Dr Robertson, the Cambridge Area Medical Officer, to let him know what our plans were and in July he convened a more formal meeting with wide representation from Papworth and Addenbrooke's. No decisions were made but further information on possible demand on resources, an appreciation of cost effectiveness and selection of patients was sought. In a lengthy letter of 20th August, I replied to these as best I could.

In the second half of the 1970s some progress was made in defining brain-death, and in January 1977 a two-year research project was started for finding the best way of preserving and storing hearts once they had been removed from the donor. As English said:

We eventually perfected a technique of combining hypo-thermic and pharmacological inhibition of metabolism of the donor heart which preserved function despite long periods of anoxic arrest; certainly long enough to con-template transporting donor hearts from anywhere in the United Kingdom to Papworth with confidence.

He went on to say:

Also of importance during the same year was the appoint-ment of Michael Petch as third Consultant Cardiologist to Papworth and Addenbrooke's. I had known Michael when I was Senior Registrar at the National Heart Hospital in 1971 and was delighted when he agreed to provide cardiological support to the transplant programme and share with me the selection of potential recipients referred from outside the Region. The agreement here was that we would see the patients independently and only accept the patient if we both agreed that transplantation was indicated. I should add that his participation came despite considerable pres-sure from Dr Wainwright Evans not to become involved.

1978 was a frustrating year as no donor organs became available. However, 1979 was different and proved to be very exciting. It is best told by Terence English:

[W]hereas 1978 was a very frustrating year, that all changed in 1979. It started with an article in the *Medical Journal* from Dr Shumway's group in Stanford, reviewing experience with their first 150 patients of whom 70 per cent survived one year with an attrition rate of 5 per cent per annum thereafter. This was accompanied by a leading article, which was cautiously supportive of cardiac transplantation. The next day, on 14th January, with Professor Calne out of town, his senior registrar Paul McMaster let me know that he had received permission for both heart and kidneys to be used from a donor in Addenbrooke's. The heart and blood group was suitable for one of our potential recipients, Charles McHugh, who had by then spent a prolonged time in Papworth and was seriously ill. We decided to go ahead with the transplant and I did the donor operation with Paul McMaster at Addenbrooke's while David Cooper, my Senior Registrar, started the recipient operation at Papworth. Just after I had removed the heart from the donor I was telephoned by Don Bethune, the Consultant Anaesthetist in charge of the recipient operation, to say that the patient had had a cardiac arrest and although he had been resuscitated and rapidly placed on cardiopulmonary bypass, he could not be sure that he had not suffered a degree of brain damage. Given the circumstances I decided that the only course was to go ahead and, having done so, the rest of the recipient operation went smoothly and the donor heart worked beautifully after it had been transplanted. Two days later, John Edwards, the Regional Press Officer, arranged a Press Conference, which was held at Addenbrooke's. This was attended by Dr Michael Petch, Dr Donald Robertson (the Area Medical Officer), and me. The degree of interest was intense and it was painful to have to express my concern that the patient, who was doing well in every other respect, had not yet recovered normal brain function. In the event he never did and as this entailed keeping him on a ventilator for prolonged periods, he inevitably developed an associated fungal infection and died 17 days after his transplant. Naturally this came as a huge disappointment, but having been given permission by the Chairman of the Area Health Authority to use our existing facilities and resources for two transplants, after which we would have to secure funds from elsewhere for the continuation of a programme, we decided to go ahead with a second case if a donor could be found.

I had a difficult meeting with Roy Calne five days after the transplant. He was very critical of what had happened and although he did not know all the facts this did not deter him from declaring that I had set back cardiac transplantation in Britain by five years. I reiterated that I felt he could still have an important role in the programme but that I was convinced that the bulk of the clinical work could only be done at Papworth. I also expressed my concern that if the current division between us was made known it would be bad for both our reputations and, more unfortunate, our proposals would be unlikely to get the blessing of the Department of Health, but that I would try and carry on.

The Transplant Advisory Panel (TAP) was due to meet on 9th February, ten days after Mr McHugh's death. The failure of his operation had drawn a lot of criticism from all sorts of quarters, both lay and professional, and I was invited to attend the TAP to 'tell members of the Panel about the case and inform them of our future plans'. As anticipated it proved a difficult meeting as although there was support from some members of the Panel, Professor Calne declared, 'that until the problems posed by the separation of the cardiac facilities at Papworth Hospital from Addenbrooke's were overcome, Cambridge was unsuitable for the setting up of a cardiac transplant programme'. The Chairman, Sir Henry Yellowlees, said that this was a problem for local resolution, and although the panel was generally supportive of the concept of establishing and funding a programme, the Chief Medical Officer reaffirmed that 'Ministers did not consider that the diversion of NHS resources to such a programme would be justified at this stage'. However, a few days later, I was much gratified to receive an encouraging letter from Professor John Goodwin, Senior Cardiologist at the Hammersmith Hospital and member of the TAP, saying that, 'of course transplantation must go on in Cambridge. It seems to me that Papworth is the right place, and I do hope the Calne problem can be sorted out'. In responding to him

I concluded, 'Certainly I can see no way that the work could be successfully pursued anywhere other than where the cardiologists, cardiac surgeons and anaesthetists normally practise. In the meantime we shall carry on in the belief that we have tried to act responsibly and that the most effective answer to the criticism would be the accomplishment of a few successful cases'.

On 24th March I wrote again to Roy Calne informing him that we had accepted another potential recipient and, recognising that he was going to be away for four weeks, asked whether he would be agreeable to Paul McMaster helping me secure the heart if a suitable donor became available in Addenbrooke's as I assumed no liver transplants would be done during his absence. He responded two days later that he and his colleagues remained very worried 'at the effect that requesting for heart donation may have on our kidney donation' and that therefore 'unless the relatives of a potential donor specifically request that the heart is used for transplantation, we should not be involved in trying to get hearts'.

And so things remained in deadlock. Dr Robertson (Area Medical Officer) visited the Department of Health to try and find out on what basis the DHSS would or would not approve a programme and I wrote to Sir John Butterfield, Regius Professor of Physic, to seek his good offices in asking Sir Henry Yellowlees to deputise a few members of the TAP, to make site visits to both Addenbrooke's and Papworth and then make a recommendation based on their findings as to where the work should be pursued. Sir John used his formidable diplomatic skills to try and mediate an agreement between Roy Calne and me but as I remained insistent that the work could only be carried out at Papworth, although I agreed to Roy assisting with both donor and recipient operations and with advice on immunosuppression, Roy's position became more entrenched and a policy was established that his team would not remove kidneys if I obtained permission for removal of the heart.

However on 18 August a donor became available in R.A.F. Ely Hospital, whose parents specifically asked that all possible organs should be used for transplantation. Roy Calne was out of town, but this enabled Paul McMaster to secure the eyes, kidneys, pancreas and heart for transplantation. Our recipient was Keith Castle, a 52-year-old builder from Wandsworth in London who we had accepted after assessment some six weeks earlier. He was not an ideal transplant candidate in that he was a heavy smoker with a history of a chronic duodenal ulcer and established peripheral vascular disease as well as his coronary disease. But in every other respect one could not have had a better patient and he subsequently became the best possible advertisement for cardiac transplantation, except that is for his inability to give up smoking entirely. Both donor and recipient operation proceeded smoothly and his postoperative recovery was for the most part uncomplicated.

By the time Keith Castle left Papworth he had already become somewhat of a national figure and remained so for the duration of the five and a half years of his subsequent life. Soon after his operation I was able to announce that funding obtained from the National Heart Research Fund would cover the extra costs of the next six patients. This was based on work done with Tom Shipp, Treasurer of the Cambridge Area Health Authority (during which I was surprised to find out how little was known about the cost of what was involved in our work at Papworth) and was in keeping with the original agreement that the Area Health Authority would only be responsible for funding the first two cases. This helped to mollify some of the more critical members of the Authority.

And then later in the year, due to the wise and persistent diplomacy of John Butterfield, agreement was reached as to how Roy Calne and I might collaborate in the future. In essence it was accepted that the clinical work could not be done at Addenbrooke's but that he would become involved with both donor and recipient operations. Also that he would advise on immunosuppression and that we would work towards introducing a cyclosporin-based regime in 6 to 18 months.

On the 22nd November we transplanted Andrew Barlow, a 29-year-old man with advanced coronary disease, with Roy Calne assisting. This operation also went smoothly and Andrew duly left hospital much improved and was soon leading a virtually normal life. That same month the Transplant Advisory Panel met again and after receiving cost estimates for a programme of eight transplants per year prepared by the Department using data from our first two cases which amounted to £17,300 per patient per first year, noted 'that results at Papworth had shown that heart transplantation was a viable proposition with a potential future and confirmed their view that the hospital complied with the criteria for a planned programme of development'. This opinion was then transmitted to the Secretary of State for Health for his approval and decision on funding.

'Getting a kick out of life'

Perhaps needless to say, the British press loved it all. On 19 August 1979 the *Sunday Telegraph* wrote a large article on its front page under the heading:

5½-HOUR HEART OPERATION
Transplant patient 'satisfactory'

The *Daily Express* showed a picture of a smiling Keith Castle with a large headline:

BEAT THAT! First picture of the heartiest man in Britain this morning

On 27 October the *Daily Telegraph* showed a photograph of Castle leaving Papworth Hospital at the top of its front page with the headline:

Heart swap man was 'fit as a fiddle'

On 10 November the *Daily Mail* showed a picture of Castle kicking a football underneath the heading:

Getting a kick out of life!

In January 1980, when Nigel Olney received a heart from a sixteen-year-old girl, Papworth's fourth heart transplant, the press again leapt on to the drama. The whole of *The Sun*'s front page told the story under the headlines:

> CAROL, 16, GIVES HEART TO A DYING MAN
> *Dramatic plane dash by transplant team*

The Guardian was more subdued but nevertheless wrote an article at the top of its front page under the heading:

> *Sitting up, with a new heart*

On 14 March 1980 the *Cambridge Evening News* was able to announce:

> Papworth Hospital scored its most remarkable success to date yesterday when it won the right to be the country's only Government-funded heart transplant centre.

Papworth had already been given £300,000 (nearly £2.5 million in today's money) by David Robinson, who had made a fortune out of his company, Robinson Rentals, which rented television sets. By this time, with the grant of £100,000 from Whitehall, Papworth Hospital was able to improve its operating theatres and add other equipment for heart operations.

While Papworth was receiving nationwide publicity for its heart transplants, the *Hunts Post* wrote articles spelling out the other heart and lung surgery which the hospital was doing. For example, in the six years leading up to August 1979 no fewer than 1,203 open-heart operations had been performed on patients with an age range of two to 78, with a success rate of nearly 95 per cent.

The articles said that great progress had been achieved in the field of heart, lung and oesophageal surgery. Age groups had been extended to include the elderly in particular and chest surgery was now giving hope and independence to many who previously would have been invalids. Young children were also benefiting by receiving corrective surgery. Their parents were encouraged to stay with them in the hospital. Operations performed were to correct congenital defects, such as a hole in the heart, and acquired heart diseases such as angina and valves damaged by rheumatic fever.

In order to provide the necessary continuous care, there were four teams of nurses, each headed by a sister, supplemented by part-time day and night staff. They served the two highly skilled cardiac surgeons and four consultant anaesthetists plus a team of doctors, technicians, radiographers, physiotherapists and laboratory staff, with great dedication.

Nursing care was provided by a team which placed patient welfare, including the reduction of anxiety, high on its list of priorities. With this expansion of the nursing activities to cope with heart and lung operations as well as tuberculosis, extra nursing courses were organised.

At the end of 1981, two and a half years after the first heart transplant at Papworth, Terence English summed up the progress made in an article for *Sterile World*:

Transplantation of the Heart

The fundamental problems of heart transplantation are similar to those posed by transplantation of other organs of the body. These comprise the selection of potential recipients, the availability of an adequate supply of suitable donor organs, the preservation of functional integrity of the donor organ between the time of excision and its revascularization in the new host, and then, after operation, the twin goals of prevention of rejection and infection. The latter two complications are inextricably interrelated and account for most of the early and late morbidity and mortality.

Results at Papworth

During the two and a half years between January 1979 and July 1981 22 patients have received heart transplants at Papworth Hospital. Their ages ranged from 16 to 52 (mean 36) years and all but one were male. Ten patients had cardiomyopathies and twelve ischaemic heart disease. The ages of the donors varied from 16 to 35 (mean 21) years. Seven were female and fifteen male. Donor hearts were brought to Papworth by road in six cases and by a combination of road and air transport in sixteen cases. The total donor heart ischaemic time varied from 108 to 205 minutes (mean 160). Early function of the transplanted heart was excellent in all cases.

By the end of July 1981 fifteen of the 22 patients were alive one month to two years after transplantation. Five patients have been investigated one year after operation and were shown angiographically to have normal left ventricular function and normal coronary arteriograms. Of the seven deaths, four have died from rejection (at 51, 59, 76, and 222 days), one from a dysrhythmia (at 131 days) and two from infection secondary to brain damage (at 17 and 64 days). No grafts have been lost due to rejection in the first six weeks after transplantation and major infection complications have been relatively uncommon.

The quality of life for the 12 survivors who have been discharged from hospital has been greatly improved, and most are delighted with the degree of rehabilitation obtained.

Coronary artery disease is now a major cause of mortality in developed countries and in the United Kingdom accounts for approximately 160,000 deaths per annum. Many of these occur suddenly and without warning and, until there is greater understanding concerning the cause and prevention of the disease, there is little hope of preventing these fatalities. Some patients who present initially with angina pectoris may be helped by coronary bypass graft surgery and in selected instances this may not only relieve symptoms but also improve life expectancy. Other patients, however, become disabled by heart failure as a result of multiple myocardial infarctions and here the ventricular damage may be so severe and diffuse that conventional cardiac surgical procedures have nothing to offer. These patients may become completely housebound as a result of fluid retention and breathlessness and it is amongst this group of patients, with irreversibly damaged left ventricles and cardiac failure, unresponsive to further medical therapy, that replacement of the heart by either a mechanical device or a transplant becomes the only conceivable solution. Clearly some patients will prefer to let life take its course and decline either option. Others, however, and particularly those with young families will seize the opportunity of a return to a more normal existence, even if the extent and duration of rehabilitation cannot be accurately predicted.

Only the future will decide which of these two methods of heart substitution will be the most successful. In the meantime it would seem reasonable that both avenues should be explored. Experimental experience with mechanical heart substitutes has so far been bedevilled by problems with the power source and with bio-incompatibility of the materials used causing blood damage. On the other hand, the effectiveness of orthotopic heart transplantation as an operative technique is firmly established and it is gratifying to see how critically ill patients can be transformed, sometimes within a matter of days, by restoration of a normal cardiac output. However, there then remains the fundamental problem of how to prevent rejection of the transplanted organ. The presently available immuno-suppressive agents are not always effective and, because of their relative non-specificity, they all have toxic side-effects. A solution to the immunological problem, which we believe is not beyond possibility, would transform clinical cardiac transplantation by removing much of its present unpredictable outcome and by bringing it within the realms of cost-effectiveness.

Following the difficulties experienced after the first two heart transplants, attempts were made to resolve the financial and location problems. Terence English said later:

> The story behind the [David] Robinson bequest was an interesting one. David Robinson was a local Cambridge millionaire who had already provided £17 million to found Robinson College. He was also a great recluse. Pauline Burnett, Chairman of the Area Health Authority had suggested that I approach him for help with funding and I did so without much expectation of success and with great difficulty in getting the application to him. I heard nothing from him for several weeks and then on returning home late one evening from work, I heard my eldest daughter, then aged 12, saying into the telephone, 'No, you cannot possibly speak to Daddy unless you tell me who you are'. I took the phone and a voice said, 'Is that you Mr English?' and after confirming that it was me, the voice said, 'You are a very difficult man to get hold of, Mr English'. On being told who I was speaking to, I could only reply, 'But Mr Robinson, you are far more difficult to get hold of'. There was a short chuckle from the other end and then an appointment made to see him and his secretary, Miss Umney, at his hideaway in Newmarket woods three days later. At that meeting the chemistry was right and before leaving they had agreed to support my application for £150,000 per annum for the two years, 1981 and 1982.

There were constant problems about funding, but on 15 October 1982 *The Times* was able to announce:

350k for heart transplant hospitals

The immediate threat to Britain's heart transplantation programme was lifted yesterday when the Department of Health announced grants of £350,000 [£1.75 million in today's money] for 1983 to Papworth Hospital in Cambridge and Harefield Hospital in Middlesex.

And on 2 February 1984:

More NHS cash for heart transplants

The government is to renew its funding for Britain's controversial heart transplant programme after evidence that costs are beginning to fall and the survival rate is improving.

The extra funding will allow the programmes to continue. So far there have been about 149 heart transplants at the two centres of whom 95 are still alive.

Since then there have been many more transplants. At the time of writing this was the position:

Transplants to date
Heart – 1,367
Heart and lung – 353
Bilateral lung – 396
Single lung – 224

Chapter 4

CONTROVERSIES

Death for transplant purposes
Panorama
'Staff crisis'

Death for transplant purposes

At the beginning of 1978, in a note to hospital doctors, the Chief Medical Officer for Health made the following observations:

> The conclusion that respiration and a beating heart are maintained solely by mechanical means and that brain death has occurred is reached entirely independently of any transplant considerations. It must remain absolutely clear that this is so.
>
> However, once the diagnosis of death has been made, the actual moment at which a respirator is switched off may be influenced by the need to maintain the kidneys or other organs in the best possible condition before they are removed for an eventual transplant. This will remain a matter for the judgment of the doctor in clinical charge of the potential donor.

One further development of significance occurred in January 1979, when the Conference of Medical Royal Colleges and their Faculties concluded that it was reasonable to equate brain death with the death of the patient.

Once again, the report which followed was a fine example of brevity and clarity.

> Whatever the mode of its production, brain death represents the stage at which a patient becomes truly dead, because by then all functions of the brain have permanently and irreversibly ceased. It is not difficult or illogical in any way to equate this with the concept

in many religions of the departure of the spirit from the body.

In October 1980, by which time the team at Papworth had for over eighteen months been removing hearts from brain-dead donors whose circulation was still intact, considerable doubt was cast by the BBC television programme *Panorama* on the whole concept of brain death as it had been defined in these documents. (See page 135 below.) None of the four cases shown was from the United Kingdom and none, according to English, would in any way have met the British criteria for the diagnosis of brain death.

Following this programme there was a significant fall in referral of organs for transplantation, particularly kidneys, and it took about a year and a half and a considerable amount of discussion before confidence was restored. When challenged, those who had criticised the criteria were unable to produce a single case in which the requirements had been fulfilled and yet the patient survived.

While Terence English never became personally involved in asking for a heart – 'the question of organ donation comes up quite independently of anything that we do' – he knew that immense tact was needed as far as the sensitivities of the relatives were concerned:

I think for the most part this is accomplished successfully. Often the matter is handled by experienced nurses on intensive care units rather than by doctors, and I do not think any relatives are put under any pressure over this, or, if they are, those instances must be very, very rare.

Of course it is the relatives who are in legal possession of the body and who can determine what is done with that body. If they do not wish the organs to be used for transplantation, even though the deceased patient carried a donor card, then they can, at the moment, overrule any wish that might have been expressed in this regard, and I believe that this is the way it should be.

As we have seen, one of the cardiologist consultants who worked at Papworth Hospital for many years, Dr David Wainwright Evans, was critical of heart transplants. A forthright Welshman, he was not slow in making his views known, not only within the hospital but to the Health Authority. He wrote in a memorandum:

The procurement of organs for transplantation, as currently practised, is unethical on several counts:

To be capable of continuing function in different bodies, organs must be removed from donors' bodies while they are still alive. So-called 'brain stem dead' patients who are designated as organ donors are self-evidently alive. This is obvious to parents who are asked for permission to remove their son's organs while – mechanical ventilation being continued – he remains in that state. Finding him warm, reactive and respiring, still perfused by his naturally beating heart, they find it difficult to accept that he is regarded as already dead by those preparing to operate upon him – to procure the wanted organs – with no change in his condition apart from drug-induced paralysis to facilitate the surgery. It should occasion no surprise that many parents, faced with that request, refuse their permission – particularly those who have been fully and frankly informed about the possibility of remaining brain function which it is beyond the power of the clinical tests routinely used to detect.

Many doctors (and philosophers) do not accept that patients who meet the UK 'brain stem death' criteria – or the various 'brain death' criteria in other countries – are dead. They acknowledge that those patients are, indeed, manifestly alive. In terms of the usual concept of death – the absence of all signs of life – such patients cannot reasonably be diagnosed and certified as dead. Most of the world's doctors would not, or could not, certify them dead. The more conservative members of the medical profession are not prepared to certify death until there are not only no remaining signs of life but also positive signs of death.

Nevertheless, there are some doctors who continue to be willing to certify those clearly living patients dead as a legally necessary preliminary to removal of their organs for transplantation. They do so on the basis of the simple bedside tests prescribed (in the UK by the Department of Health in its Code of Practice) despite the increasing body of evidence that they are inadequate for the purpose. When introduced, over 30 years ago, those tests were claimed to have the power to diagnose death of the brain – it being tacitly assumed that 'brain death', as clinically diagnosed, would be a generally acceptable basis for certifying death while the body remained alive – but that claim was clearly spurious, most of the brain not being tested at all (or, indeed, testable) and the prescribed tests lacking the power even to diagnose death of the brain stem as a matter of fact. The fallacy of that initial claim was formally recognized in 1955 but the certification of death for transplant purposes has continued on essentially the same clinical assessment, albeit on a novel conceptual basis which, insofar as it has been debated at all, has not found wide philosophical acceptance.

This new concept of human death is comprised of only two elements – the irreversible loss of the capacity to breathe spontaneously and the irreversible loss of the capacity for consciousness. It was claimed – without presentation of evidence in support – that death of the brain stem sufficed to ensure those permanent losses and that the prescribed tests sufficed to establish death of the brain stem. There is, in fact, no sound scientific evidence to support those claims. The prescribed test for irreversible loss of ventilatory function (breathing) is dangerous but not sufficiently stringent, and there is no means of testing for residual capacity for consciousness. Consciousness is not understood. The notion that its arousal depends crucially and exclusively on elements of the brain stem looks increasingly insecure in light of recent neuroscientific observations. Those elements are, in any case, not specifically testable. They can be said to be permanently functionless only by implication, i.e. when it is certain that the whole of the brain stem is truly dead – a state which it is beyond the power of the prescribed tests to establish.

The most plausible basis for the continuing certification of 'death for transplant purposes' on the diagnostic criteria currently in use is that they are widely believed to suffice for the purpose of forecasting death – the final cessation of blood circulation and respiration (plus the passage of a sufficiently long period of time) – within a few hours or days, despite the continuation of mechanical ventilation and other life-support measures. That is of course, in reality, their use as prognostic guidelines. But their confusion with criteria for the actual diagnosis of death is essential to current organ transplantation practice and is backed by the Department of Health in the Code of Practice which governs those procedures. It may be that the doctors involved come to terms with this inappropriate use on the premise that, although the patients they certify dead on that basis are not de facto dead, it doesn't matter because they have no chance of recovery. This is the utilitarian view – that they are 'dead enough' for transplant purposes and that it is in some distorted sense 'unethical' to await de facto death because to do so would render the wanted organs unviable. But it ignores the inescapable fact that, as the donor is not really dead – whatever his status on paper – he is killed by the operation for removal of his organs.

If there is to be a truly ethical basis for the procurement of organs for transplantation, there must first be a fully and frankly informed public discussion and debate about the various options capable of providing organs in a viable state for the purpose. In practice – because procurement from living, healthy donors offends against the fundamental 'first, do no harm' principle, and organs taken from unequivocally dead people are no good for

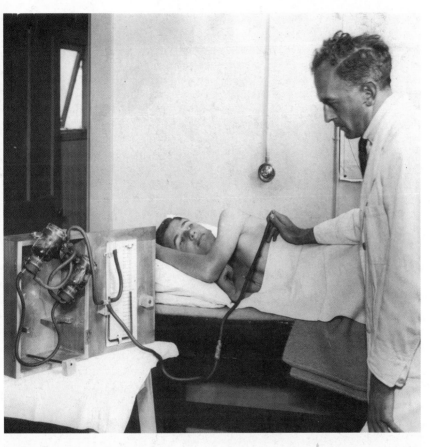

Pneumothorax – a special machine invented by R.M.O. Hall at Papworth.

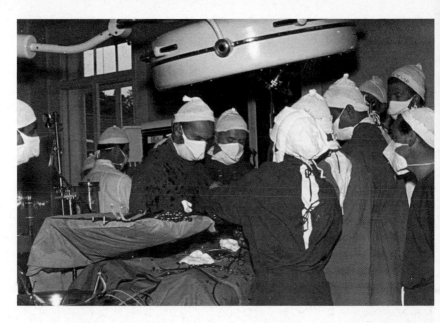

Operation in progress at Papworth.

Nurses by the pond at Papworth.

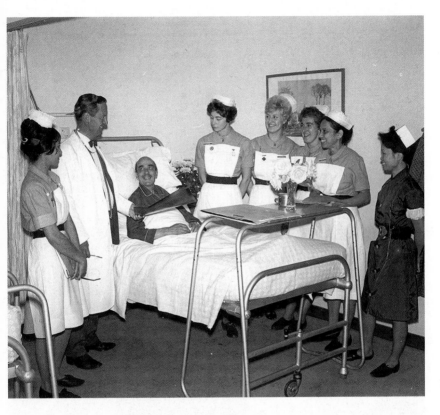

Christopher Parish with six nurses and a patient.

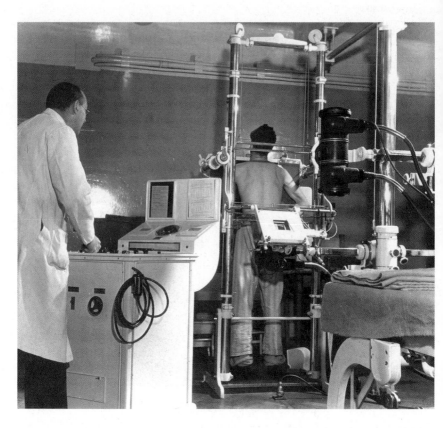

The X-ray department, which was always busy. In one year 7,156 films of 5,703 patients were taken.

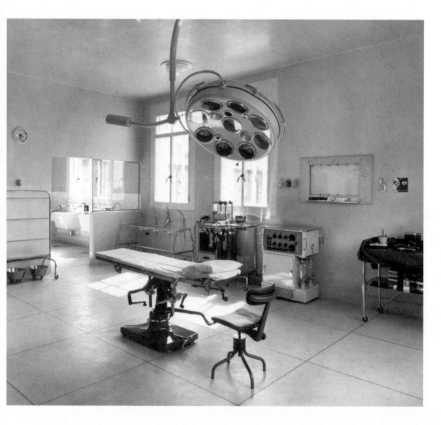

Operating theatre at Papworth.

HRH Queen Elizabeth during a visit to Papworth.

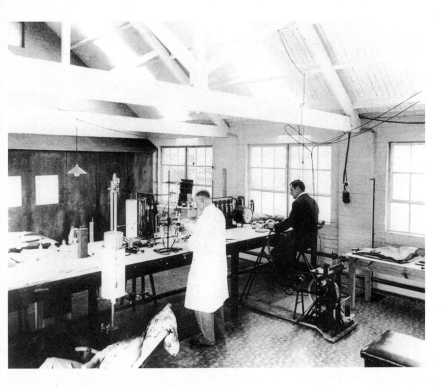

Research in
the Papworth
laboratory.

Dr E.M. Cheffins, a consultant
physician at Papworth.

Scottish dancers at a fundraising party in the grounds at Papworth.

Charles Hubbard, a key theatre superintendent at Papworth.

transplantation – these are limited to the acquisition of organs from the dying. It may be that, when all the relevant facts have been made clearly and universally known, without obfuscation or concealment, some people will be willing to allow removal of their organs for the sake of others when they are, as certainly as can be known in the current state of medical practice, doomed to die soon. Consent to donation on that fully informed basis would seem to constitute an ethically valid offer if the legal difficulties could be overcome.

Until we can be sure that everybody who might be used as an organ donor has fully understood the nature of that procedure, it cannot be presumed that they have consented to such use merely because they have not registered objection. In the present state of public knowledge about transplant procedures, we are clearly very far from being able to make that assumption of universal comprehension and approval.

Wainwright Evans caused considerable anguish within Papworth Hospital itself, as can be seen by these parts of letters between him and other surgeons.

In his letter to Ben Milstein on 24 March 1982, Wainwright Evans wrote:

I am very sorry that you saw fit to write me such a high-handed letter about this matter. I had sought a discussion with you, by word of mouth in the corridor recently and via what I thought was a tactful letter in reply to the one Frank Wells sent me, and I feel it would have been much better if you had allowed us to sort things out on that basis.

We have now, thanks to a chance meeting this morning, had an opportunity for a fairly protracted discussion of the problem and I think you understand that, if you cannot give me an assurance that patients I refer to you will not end up in the care of one of your colleagues who practises transplantation, I shall be unable to continue referring patients to you.

And Milstein felt it necessary to write to Wainwright Evans:

Frank Wells has passed to me your letter of 17th March in which you complained about the proposal to review Mr Southgate in John Wallwork's clinic. This is not an administrative error.

Incidentally, when you have matters of this nature about which you wish to make observations, I would be grateful if you would address your complaint direct to me and not via my junior staff. I think it is unseemly, undignified and unfair for them to have to be involved.

On 13 September 1982 Wainwright Evans also wrote to *The Times*:

Questioning view of heart transplants
The opposition of the three Papworth consulting cardiologists to human cardiac transplantation has been the subject of recent press reports. The inaccuracy of some

of these persuades me to offer the following facts and observations.

The letter formally expressing our disapproval was sent to Mr Terence English on March 19 1982. We have not received a reply. That letter was certainly not the occasion for my first expression of opposition which has been consistent from before the start of his work at Papworth. Of the two other signatories, Dr Hugh Fleming and Dr Michael Petch, the latter has given some of his reasons at the time of his withdrawal from the programme in August 1980.

Our letter did not rehearse the basis of our objections. These include, clinical, ethical, scientific, financial and resource considerations. Unlike renal transplantation, cardiac transplantation necessitates acceptance of the 'brain-death' concept and its equation with death.

Although never tested by controlled trial, it may be that satisfaction of the British Brain Death criteria suffices to predict that the patient will die within the next few days. However, their satisfaction does not mean that there is, at that time, no life in the brain. Indeed, relatively simple further tests, such as an electro encephalography would if applied demonstrate persistent activity in the brains of some of these unfortunates.

To regard such patients as brain-dead has always seemed to me scientifically and semantically incorrect ...

While I do not share your Science Editor's view that the cardiac transplantation argument is primarily about money, it is interesting to note (*Cambridge Evening News*, Sept 3) that the Papworth transplantation programme is estimated to have cost £646,735 [nearly £4 million in today's money] so far whereas the donated money which is supposed to have paid for it amounts to only £400,000. Approval for the programme was understood to be conditional upon its making no extra charge in the strained local health budget.

Another person who made life difficult for Terence English in pursuing his heart transplant operations was Roy Calne, as is clear from this letter he wrote in his capacity as Professor of Surgery at Addenbrooke's Hospital:

Dear Terence,

Thank you for your letter explaining about your new potential recipient for a heart transplant. I have had consultation with my colleagues and we are very worried at the effect of requesting for heart donation may have on our kidney donation, particularly when my department is not involved in the heart transplantation programme and I personally disapprove of the way it is being done.

I therefore feel that unless the relatives of a potential donor specifically request that the heart be used for transplantation we should not be involved in trying to get hearts. I am sorry to appear unhelpful in this way but I do feel it is wrong for heart transplantation to progress at Papworth, completely divorced from the main organ transplant programme in Cambridge.

Yours sincerely,

R.Y. CALNE

Furthermore, one of the key members of the transplant team withdrew from the team after writing this letter to Terence English:

5 August 1980

Mr T.A.H. English
Consultant Cardiothoracic Surgeon
Papworth Hospital

Dear Terence
I said that I would write to you about the role of the physician in cardiac transplantation. These thoughts have been prompted by Alan Gay's operation which disturbed me deeply. The timing of cardiac transplantation can only be a surgeon's decision and, in the end, the individual recipient will also be the surgeon's choice. The selection of recipients does not necessarily lead to surgical treatment but it is nevertheless a decision to proceed with a form of treatment which the physician cannot administer. By the time patients are referred for assessment they are already deemed beyond medical treatment by their own medical advisers. This leaves the physician associated with a programme of transplantation giving advice which is considered, respected and sometimes set aside; an uncomfortable and untenable position for an independent clinician. As in other fields of medicine physicians and surgeons will, and indeed should, disagree and the patient must be advised by one or other at any particular stage in his illness. This leads me to the conclusion that only one

person, you, should be advising potential recipients for transplantation and that I should no longer be involved in their assessment.

This change of practice is a logical one and my major anxiety is that other people will construe it as meaning that you and I have fallen out. However, I do not think we should spend too much time worrying about that but concentrate on the more important issue which is the effect on the programme. I believe that any effect will be slight and that the administration of potential recipients will be easier for you. I know that you have found my opinion most helpful and I believe that part of that help has been to give you someone to talk to; I also believe that Richard Cory-Pearce will be able to take over this role. My help is not essential and it is ironical that two of our best patients, David Williams and Nigel Olney, were transplanted without my assessment. One point that does concern me is that you may be tempted to operate on someone too early in their illness and I think that you should counter this temptation by asking the referring cardiologist, on each occasion, if he really considers that his patient has no alternative.

Another practical consequence of this line of thought is the supervision of the medical registrar who is to help in the programme. I do not think that we should ask a man to be responsible to both of us. The job is not a simple service one and there will be difficult decisions about his work where you and I will not agree. The sensible solution is to reconsider this post, presumably in consultation with the British Heart Foundation, and to ask whether a surgical registrar might not be more appropriate?

Cardiac transplantation generates different and novel problems; that is its attraction. But it is a surgical procedure and the physician's role is a subsidiary one. You have always treated my views with courtesy and respect and I know that you will continue to do so. However, the nature of the work does not allow two clinicians to have an equal say nor can I see how this can be accomplished. I do not believe that I should continue in my present role which, to say the least, is making me feel most uncomfortable and I will, therefore, stop seeing patients admitted for assessment.

With best wishes

Yours sincerely

Mike

M.C. Petch
Consultant Cardiologist

After his withdrawal Michael Petch made little comment, but after two years he felt he needed to give his true reasons for withdrawing to answer the often inaccurate comments made by others:

My decision to withdraw from Papworth Hospital's transplant programme was not taken lightly. I knew it would be misinterpreted. I knew it might jeopardise the programme. But, having taken the decision, I felt as if a burden had been lifted from me – a subconscious vindication.

Papworth Hospital, set alongside Ermine Street, might have been well placed for Roman traffic accidents but its situation presents the twentieth century cardiologist with problems, because outpatients, coronary care, nuclear medicine and the clinical school are all 15 miles away, in Cambridge. Despite that, and contrary to press reports, the hospital provides an amicable and efficient inpatient service for Cambridge and East Anglian folk with diseases of the heart and chest.

Patients come from their general practitioners and local physicians to the cardiologists and chest physicians who are supported by their colleagues in radiology, pathology, surgery and anaesthetics. Most cardiac disorders are resolved before the patient ever reaches Papworth. Even then, three quarters of the patients admitted to the regional cardiac unit (1,498 last year) are helped without recourse to cardiac surgery.

Although the heart transplant programme has never represented more than 2 to 3 per cent of the hospital's work, there are good reasons for having it: the existence of young people dying from intractable heart failure, the satisfactory results from Stanford, the official approval of brain death, the ability to store and transport hearts safely, the more accurate diagnosis of cardiac rejection by biopsy, and the fact that kidney and liver transplants are established in Cambridge.

My objections to the programme are on medical, moral, scientific and administrative grounds.

Some young people with myocardial failure slowly become cachexic and die despite full medical treatment. They need new hearts. Most do not behave like this but deteriorate unpredictably, often with spontaneous remission and occasionally with dramatic improvement after simple medical measures like bed rest or vasodilator therapy.

Medical misgivings

Many victims of 'terminal' heart failure live reasonable, albeit sedentary, lives for months or years before suddenly succumbing to ventricular fibrillation, a fact that is not sufficiently appreciated. Any cardiologist selecting recipients for cardiac transplantation must know his patient very well before recommending surgery.

Once a patient has entertained the idea of a new heart it becomes more difficult to say 'no'. The selectors are exposed to other subtle pressures too; for example, a man investigated with a view to left ventricular aneurysmectomy moves from being a human and medical problem to a surgical and technical one. The question is not what is best for him, but what operation might help him.

In addition, a transplanter is bound to be an enthusiast for his operation and will want a waiting list of patients with differing blood groups and so on. He may also feel, as I did, an obligation to treat at least 10 cases a year in order to fulfil the Health Department requirement of a proper programme.

Only the patient's cardiologist can decide on the suitability of cardiac transplantation. But he must be careful, particularly if he is being pressed by the family. He must resist the temptation to refer his patient in order to get rid of a difficult problem. He must not fall into the medical trap of thinking that doing something's better than doing nothing. And he must acquaint himself with the complications.

On waking after a heart transplant the recipient feels wonderful. This honeymoon lasts only until the rigours of the postoperative regime are established – isolation, careful monitoring, cardiac biopsies, immunosuppression, investigation and early treatment of any suspicious lesion which might herald the beginning of a fatal illness. It is quite unlike normal medicine, where masterly inactivity is often best, or renal transplantation, where irreversible rejection may be treated by dialysis. All recipients have at least one complication, ranging from the distressingly fatal to the relatively trivial: fortunately these seem to have been less troublesome since the introduction of Cyclosporin A.

About a third of recipients die in the first year after transplantation, usually as a result of rejection. I found these complications difficult to accept because they were a consequence of the treatment that I had recommended rather than a natural consequence of the original disease. I can remember a handful of patients who owe their lives to the operation. I am delighted for them. But I have another memory of a man who reconciled himself to dying, saw a chance of survival only to find that chance denied him when a new heart was not forthcoming. He and his kind need to be entered on the balance sheet. There are a few, and they are probably very few, memorable patients who might benefit from cardiac transplantation.

Moral and scientific aspects
Organ transplantation is made possible by the death of another previously healthy person. Any form of treatment that starts from this point will never be an unqualified success.

I find the concept of brain death acceptable although I would like to see a list of doctors and hospitals entrusted to make the diagnosis. But I do dislike the idea of removing a beating heart. I know this is illogical. I cannot explain it. My sensibility is shared by some physicians and for us it is a virtue, in different circumstances, enabling us, for example, to perceive our patients' unspoken needs.

It may be this quality that makes doctors reluctant to ask for organs for transplantation. We would rather leave a family alone with its brain-dead relative until his heart stops, the traditional moment of death. It does not preclude the removal of other organs afterwards.

A further macabre aspect of cardiac transplantation is the attitude of the potential recipient who looks forward to dangerous road conditions. After discussing this with one patient I drove slowly home wondering how the Government would honour its pledge to increase the number of organs for transplantation; would the seatbelt law be repealed?

Any scientific spin-off from cardiac transplantation cannot be used to justify the procedure, which must stand or fall on its merit as a form of treatment. Studies on the physiology and metabolism of the denervated heart, the effect of drugs, and the accelerated atheroma are sidelines which can be studied equally well in animals.

Advances in medical practice are usually the result of developments in other fields. Cardiologists now dilate coronary arteries with catheters, monitor pulmonary artery pressure at the bedside, use microprocessors to detect and analyse arrhythmias, insert pacemakers of amazing versatility, and employ a range of drugs capable of transforming their patients' lives.

Is this better than our present practice? The programmes at Papworth and Harefield may have extended the original Stanford experiments but, from the scientific point of view, the recent advances have been immunological: the surgical technique was worked out over a decade ago.

Suppose surgery, as we now know it, has reached its zenith? Then clearly surgeons will turn to subjects like immunology in order to satisfy their intellectual curiosity. But the immunological problems of organ rejection could be investigated equally well in renal transplantation where the medical and human difficulties are less.

Surely the future of the surgical craft will encompass artificial organs, the extension of catheter and endoscopic techniques and perhaps the use of animal organs? These are likely to be more profitable avenues of research for the cardiac surgeon. Transplantation of the human heart may well be a scientific cul-de-sac, especially since there will always be a limited number of donors.

Surgery is not a satisfactory answer to the problem of myocardial failure. Ischaemic damage is best prevented. Congenital and valve lesions should be corrected before failure occurs. Only the rare cases of primary myocardial failure need a replacement pump.

One person on whom the supporters of continuing heart transplants could rely was Norman Shumway, who wrote to *The Times* in August 1982:

Triumph of Operation Transplant

The introduction two years ago of a new and relatively non-toxic immune suppressing chemical called Cyclosporin-A has revolutionised all areas of organ transplant. 90 per cent of all patients receiving new hearts at Stanford University leave the hospital in a stable condition with excellent prospects for full rehabilitation. Similar results are now coming from the Papworth Hospital in Cambridge under the aegis of Mr Terence English and from the Harefield Hospital by Mr Magdi Yacoub.

An invention by the late Philip Caves of Glasgow provides the best measurement of the condition of the heart transplantation. A small piece of the heart is actually removed for a microscopic study and depending on the appearance of the tissue, more or less Cyclosporin-A is given to protect the transplantation from rejection of the patient from excessive immune-suppression. To date more than 750 heart transplants have been performed by 74 countries throughout the world.

Heart transplants are here to stay and heart–lung

transplants are just around the corner. Basic research and new immune suppressing medicines can only improve what is now the only hope for many patients with lethal heart and lung diseases.

The BBC's *Listener* journal summarised the challenges of Papworth's heart transplantation programme in 1982:

The most significant fact about the resumption, after a ten-year gap, of a consistent British heart transplant programme is that it began, not in a major teaching hospital, but in the rural surroundings of Papworth Everard in Cambridgeshire.

Papworth Hospital used to be a tuberculosis unit. The small, separate rooms, opening on to long lawns and a noisy duckpond, are a reminder that isolation and fresh air were the long-term remedies then. Now the enemy is chronic heart disease – and the challenge to the doctors is financially greater and politically more sensitive.

Keith Castle, second of the heart transplant patients at Papworth, describes the surgeon who gave him a new heart, Terence English, as 'the quiet man'. To borrow his own Cockney phrase, Castle is 'not a bad judge'. Terence English, who is South African born of British stock – his father was in gold mining – explained his attitude to publicity in this way: 'My hope had been, quite honestly, to say nothing, to do nothing, until the operation had been done and the patient had either left hospital or died, and only then to make an announcement. That is the way all of us at Papworth would like to have done it. We weren't allowed to under the circumstances, but I do believe that's the way we should go.'

It is a forlorn hope – in the foreseeable future. There is the controversy over whether or not scarce National Health Service funds should be allocated to work that even Terence English still describes as 'experimental'. There is the tendency for coroners to say things like: 'On ethical and moral grounds I do find the operations distasteful, and I am also uncertain as to the benefits of transplant surgery, which is still in its infancy and very expensive.' And there is the instinctive belief, paraded in song and sonnet, that, somehow, the heart is the cradle of life and love.

English remembers the furore that surrounded the last spate of heart transplants in Britain, in 1968 and 1969. He remembers the photographs of Union Jack-waving medics, smiling as if England had again won the World Cup. He knows that we remember that, too. He told me: 'I think the backlash was partly because we had so many failures … and partly because many members of the medical profession felt that the glare of publicity which had attended these operations was unfavourable, to put it kindly.' He realises that publicity could damage the current heart transplant programme: that people who are opposed to heart transplantation and find the publicity unpalatable will use it to detract from the actual work that is being done.

I asked whether he feared another backlash when the patients died – as, going by history, they surely would.

'I am very aware that this could happen. The patients alive at present are all doing well for their particular stage after the operation. I'm aware of the danger of a false sense of euphoria developing. If we lose a couple of patients, then it would depend a little bit how they died. But we would look forward to the long-term analysis of our results. If, after four or five years, we can approach the results that have been achieved at Stanford to date, then we will be satisfied.'

Stanford University, California, is the yardstick by which everything the Papworth team attempts is judged. They follow the same patterns of drugs to suppress the rejection of the new heart. They attach the same importance to high standards of nursing and after-care. They have the same approach to publicity – for, beside Stanford's Dr Norman Shumway, Terence English is a bubbling extrovert.

English has twice visited Stanford. More important, he was a contemporary and good friend of the late Philip Caves, a protégé of Shumway's, who came back to Britain, worked prodigiously as a cardiac surgeon in Glasgow and Edinburgh, and died two years ago at the tragically early age of 38. English and Caves often talked of resuming transplants in Britain. Had Caves lived, heart transplants might now have been going on in Scotland rather than in Cambridge and London, English says:

'We agreed that the only way we could get the programme started was to show we could do the operation properly and we staked a great deal, therefore, on obtaining success with our first few cases. He believed the right way to do it was to start and not stop, and if the first few patients died one should still carry on.'

It is in the figures achieved by Shumway at Stanford that English and his team find both the justification for heart transplantation and the determination to overcome all obstacles. Shumway and his colleagues have carried out more than 200 transplants over ten years. Based on 94 consecutive cases, they now offer the patient a 70 per cent chance of living one year, a 50 per cent chance of living five years. Most of these long-term patients are back at work. English speaks of Shumway's 'obsessional approach to achieving perfection in heart transplantation'. His is a similar attitude: an unequivocal determination. To the question 'Why bother to do heart transplants at all?' he replied: 'I think there is a need for them. It's a very basic answer. I think there are many people in this country, and in any developed Western country where coronary disease is prevalent, who cannot be treated in any other way.'

The Listener continued:

When patients are referred to Papworth, English likes it to be clearly understood that they are coming for a short period of assessment only. Their arrival at the hospital does not imply any commitment to transplantation either on their part or on his.

With limited resources available, it seemed reasonable to confine treatment to those who might benefit most. The upper age limit was set at 50 and the lower age limit at 15. The upper limit was raised coincidentally with the surgeons themselves reaching the age of 50.

The decision to exclude cases under 15 years was based on the view that what was wanted at the end of assessment was a well-informed patient who understood the risks and imponderables, and who could be left to make his own decision as to whether to accept transplantation or not – should he be offered it.

'We see the matter in a rather different light from the usual form of consultation that takes place between a physician and his patient in which the physician so often advises his patient to take a particular course.

'We do not take that view. We feel that because the outcome is unpredictable, the right way to do things is to make an offer which the patient can freely accept or not.

'And we feel that we cannot do this with children who might not have the experience and maturity to understand what is being offered to them. The decision would therefore have to be made by their parents, and we feel that this is something that is not ideal.'

As compliance with the postoperative management is clearly essential if the outcome is to be successful, English is at pains to ensure as far as he can that his patients have a sufficiently mature attitude and a stable home background. A comprehensive report from a social worker is always obtained, as is an independent report from a psychiatrist.

During what English describes as 'this rather leisurely assessment' the patient will spend three or four days at the hospital being interviewed by the surgical and medical staff, speaking freely with the nurses, and talking to past and present transplant patients. If he has a wife, she will usually stay in the nearby village but will spend most of her days on the ward with her husband, so that she becomes as well informed as he.

While some patients may have been told by their physicians that things will be all right eventually, even though they have, in fact, been getting worse, many know that they are likely to die soon, and this is something which English does not evade when the matter comes up, which it often does.

'One has found that the patients often regard it as a relief to be able to talk about their illness in this way, particularly in the presence of their wife, because often the wife has been told about the seriousness of the prognosis, and yet it has been suggested to her that she should not be quite so frank with her husband because it would depress him.'

'Many of these patients are depressed by the time they come to us, and it is the psychiatrist's rule to try to distinguish between those who have organic mental disease and those who have a very natural reaction to the seriousness of their illness.'

Predictably, the patients show intense interest in how a particular heart is selected for a particular patient.

'They are aware of the fact that patients who have been selected sometimes die on our waiting-list, because there are not enough hearts or facilities to treat them all, and I think they have a right to know how the system works.'

(Patients now stand a 60 per cent chance of being transplanted if they are selected on to the waiting-list.)

The waiting-list at Papworth does not often exceed eight to ten, and, when the number of possible recipients of any one heart has been whittled down to three or four on the basis of blood grouping, the heart is normally given to the patient who has been waiting the longest.

While this seems the fairest way to English and his colleagues, it is not an invariable rule. Potential recipients of new hearts are told that if the team hears of a patient who is deteriorating rapidly at another institution, then he might be given a donor heart ahead of them, even though he has only been on the waiting-list for a few weeks.

The fact that some patients will never come to transplantation and will die on the waiting-list was something that worried English a great deal at the beginning.

'However my impression has been that many of these patients have gained a considerable degree of comfort during their last few months of life through the mere fact of knowing that there was something that could still possibly help them, and this, I think, just expresses the normal human capacity for hope. This impression has been confirmed by relatives of patients who have written to me after their husband or son died to tell me that this was the way it had seemed to them.'

Turning from the recipient to the donor, English addressed himself to the following ethical questions:

Can brain death be diagnosed with certainty? Can it be equated with death of the patient?

Should the known wishes of a donor be respected in terms of trying to fulfil his desire that his organs should be used to benefit others in the event of his death?

What is the best way to respect the sensitivities of the aggrieved relatives and how should one best approach them to ask for organ donation?

Until October 1976 it might be argued that the medical profession was in some disarray over the first point. However for most people this matter was resolved with the publication of a report by the Conference of Medical Royal Colleges and their Faculties.

This beautifully concise and clear report was prompted not by any consideration of heart transplantation but by the need to manage humanely those patients with severe brain damage who were being maintained on artificial respiration by means of mechanical ventilators.

It was agreed that permanent functional death of the brain stem constituted brain death, and that once this had occurred further artificial support was fruitless and should be withdrawn. There then followed a lucid outline of the diagnostic criteria that had to be met, through relatively simple clinical tests, to decide whether brain stem death, and therefore brain death, had occurred.

Panorama

The controversy over 'brain-death' was picked up by the BBC television programme, *Panorama*, in October 1980, prompting the *New Scientist* to write:

Transplants in Britain: the destructive power of television

1981 was a mixed year for organ transplants, according to Professor Roy Calne, speaking at a recent press conference in London. It should have been an excellent year; for although it is difficult to assess the benefit of any single innovation, it did seem that cyclosporin A had significantly reduced the problem of organ rejection. At Cambridge, 80 per cent of kidneys transplanted from cadavers were still functioning after one year when protected by cyclosporin whereas with other methods of immunosuppression, a 50 per cent survival at one year is more usual with cadaver kidneys. Nine out of 12 liver transplants treated with cyclosporin A are also surviving at Cambridge, said Calne, and Professor Starzl, in Colorado, was having similar success.

However, the *Panorama* programme shown on BBC1, which suggested that transplant surgeons sometimes took organs from dead patients without absolute proof of death, had sadly compromised transplantation in Britain, said Calne. The programme, he said, was a disgrace. The 'evidence' presented was entirely for the 'prosecution' and the four examples given all came from the US – because, said Calne, there simply are no examples from Britain. In the months following the programme eight out of ten people at Cambridge refused permission for organs to be removed from their dead relatives whereas in the previous 16 years refusals were practically unknown. 'Most people were glad to think that the death of a relative had at least benefited some other sick person,' said Calne.

Professor Calne estimated 'conservatively' that 100 patients had died as a direct result of the *Panorama* programme. Patients on dialysis were not able to have transplants because of lack of donors; and patients with renal diseases who needed dialysis were dying because the dialysis units were blocked by patients waiting for transplants. The BBC should, said Calne, be ashamed.

Instead, they seemed proud of their programme. He was, he said, appalled.

In addition, the doctors whose job it was to discuss with relatives of the deceased the possibility of removing organs for transplantation had never relished the task. Now, faced with the likelihood that the request would be turned down, and the relatives distressed, they were reluctant even to initiate the discussion.

'Staff crisis'

Inevitably, the initial heart transplants, with all the attendant publicity, put pressure on Papworth Hospital and on 11 March 1980 the *Cambridge Evening News* published an article under the heading:

> '*STAFF CRISIS' AT PAPWORTH: Heart swaps causing backlog of work – claim.*

Apparently the claim was made by a Mrs Roberta Cannon, a member of the Cambridgeshire Health Authority:

> There are 33 children waiting on the list, and the list is increasing month by month. The nursing services are short-staffed and the senior members who bear this added burden are getting very, very tired. Are we doing anything about this?

There was an article in *The Guardian* questioning the priority given to heart transplants and its effect on other medical care. Ben Milstein was prompted to write a letter in reply to that newspaper:

Sir, Your leader writer (March 20) considers that Papworth Hospital's 'failure' is the figure of 33 children on the Papworth Cardiac Unit waiting list as reported by a local newspaper. What your leader writer seems to have failed to understand is that this waiting list is for the assessment of children who may have cardiac disease.

The children referred to are not urgent cases. The reason for their having to wait for investigation is that specialist X-ray facilities, which have never been adequate to meet the increasing demand, are required for the investigations.

The Radiologist-in-Charge wrote to the *Cambridge Evening News* on March 19, pointing this out and denying that this waiting list is significantly affected by the transplantation programme at Papworth Hospital.

You write: 'Yet the transplantations are to continue and the children to be pushed to one side. Transplantations are glamorous, valvular defects in children are not.' There is, in fact, only one child awaiting open-heart surgery. And every cardiac surgeon knows that transplant surgery is relatively simple, whereas the management of children with congenital heart disease requires far more skill and application and indeed extends the cardiac surgeon's technical and intellectual resources to the limit.

As a matter of fact, since the programme of cardiac transplantation at this hospital was started the number of open-heart cases operated per month has increased by 30 per cent. Our waiting list for urgent cases is 10 days and for non-urgent cases 8–10 weeks. This is a lower figure than for most of the 46 open-heart surgery units in the country.

It is true that our waiting list for surgical operations is increasing. The reason for this is that the high quality of the work in this unit and the low operative mortality are now becoming more widely known. Your leader writer calls this 'failure.' Most people would consider it as success. – Yours faithfully, B.B. Milstein

Chapter 5

HEART–LUNG TRANSPLANTS

First successful heart–lung transplant at Papworth
An outstanding contribution

First successful heart–lung transplant at Papworth

At the end of the 1980s John Wallwork edited, and also wrote a chapter in, a book covering all aspects of heart–lung transplantation. He wrote, in a chapter entitled 'Indications for Operation, Patient Selection and Assessment':

> Heart–lung transplantation has followed other organ transplant procedures by rapidly going through an early period of development since the first successful operation in 1982. The indication for that first operation was primary pulmonary hypertension. Since then the disease processes which can be treated by heart–lung transplantation have become more numerous and diverse than at first thought. Furthermore, the criteria for acceptance of individuals from these groups and the timing of intervention continue to change. This evolution and expansion of the scope of heart–lung transplantation will continue as more knowledge is gained of the short-, mid- and long-term results. Criteria regarded as contraindications to surgery 5 years ago are now not so regarded. For example, some patients with previous cardiac or thoracic surgery are now accepted and a major group of patients, those with cystic fibrosis, are now acceptable as potential recipients; they may indeed be one of the largest groups to benefit.

Wallwork noted that there were several conditions potentially suitable for heart–lung transplantation: Eisenmenger's syndrome, primary pulmonary hypertension, cystic fibrosis, fibrosing alveolitis, emphysema, sarcoidosis, bronchiectasis, histiocytosis X and pulmonary fibrosis.

The chapter described the indications for and assessment of patients for heart–lung transplantation, illustrated by the Papworth Hospital programme experience. It also assessed the potential need as far as could be determined from mortality data of the major disease categories at that time acceptable for heart–lung transplantation.

Indications For Surgery

The conditions potentially suitable for heart–lung transplantation were basically divided into two major groups: those patients with primary lung disease, including primary pulmonary hypertension, and those patients with secondary pulmonary hypertension due to cardiac disease. The largest group among these latter patients comprised those with congenital heart disease who might or might not have had previous surgery, but for whom there was now no anatomical or physiological chance of correction. It was among this group of patients that the majority of future expansion would take place in the development of heart–lung transplantation for infants and children. The list of potential diseases was not exhaustive. There would be many individuals with a variety of disorders which could lead to chronic cardiorespiratory failure who would be suitable for heart–lung transplantation. The three major diagnostic groups were patients with Eisenmenger's syndrome, primary pulmonary hypertension and cystic fibrosis. Patients with other forms of lung disease made up a further sizeable heterogeneous group of potential patients.

Some patients, particularly those with fibrosing lung disease, would be suitable for single lung transplantation and some patients without cardiac involvement might be suitable for double lung transplantation. All patients with Eisenmenger's syndrome, however, would need both heart and lung transplantation. It was too early in the development of these procedures to give definitive guidelines which would determine the particular procedure most suitable for those potential recipients for whom there was a possible choice of operation.

It used to be thought, for example, that one of the advantages of combined heart–lung transplantation was the ability to monitor rejection of the heart–lung bloc by way of endomyocardial biopsy. By this time they knew that this was not the case, as the lungs tended to reject prior to and without cardiac rejection. Indeed, at Papworth they had, like several other centres, abandoned routine cardiac biopsy in heart–lung transplant recipients.

There was still concern about the mid- and long-term problems of stenosis of the bronchial/tracheal anastomosis in isolated lung transplants. In heart–lung transplantation, a systemic bronchial blood supply from coronary collaterals was retained, which was not the case in isolated lung transplantation. Although satisfactory healing could be achieved, the lack of a native bronchial blood supply might be responsible for these problems.

Double lung transplantation for primary lung disease had been advocated in order to maximize donor organ supply, enabling the heart to be given to a second recipient. However, Reitz and Yacoub had introduced independently the concept of the heart of a heart–lung transplant recipient, if it was suitable, being donated to a heart transplant patient as an alternative to maximize organ usage. This procedure still maintained the benefits of transplanting the heart–lung bloc intact. The future of this development again awaited full evaluation before definite statements could be made about the most appropriate operation for the individual recipient.

Need For Heart–Lung Transplantation

The true potential need for heart–lung transplantation could only be estimated. As acceptance criteria changed, the size of the recipient pool would alter accordingly. No morbidity data were available to assess the size of the recipient population, but a minimum estimated need could be derived from the mortality data for the major disease groups in the appropriate age ranges figures for England and Wales.

The number of deaths per year was considered for each of the following major disease groups: Eisenmenger's syndrome, pulmonary hypertension, cystic fibrosis and other parenchymatous lung diseases which include cryptogenic fibrosing alveolitis and granulomatous diseases such as sarcoidosis. The annual death rates for a population of approximately 30 million people were shown for both age groups. Miscellaneous diseases of the lung accounted for the majority of the deaths, and the largest single disease group was patients with cystic fibrosis.

The deaths per year per million population of patients who could be potential heart–lung transplant recipients were 5.8 in the 5–9 year olds and 11.3 in the 10–49 age group. It had to be stressed that the potential recipient population was probably much greater than this figure when the large pool of chronically disabled patients not immediately at risk of death was taken into account. Not all of these patients would prove to be acceptable, however, because of other contraindications to surgery. At Papworth during the previous two years, 26 per cent of patients assessed had been excluded because of factors such as previous pleurectomy or high-dose steroid therapy.

The need for heart–lung transplantation undoubtedly exceeded the capacity to transplant all these patients. Some selection of patients would continue to be imposed to maximize the benefit of heart–lung transplantation to the population and minimize the risks to the individual.

The first successful heart–lung transplant in Europe was performed at Papworth Hospital and was carried out in 1984 by John Wallwork. He had been at Stanford Hospital in the USA as chief resident when Bruce Reitz carried out the world's first successful heart–lung transplantation in 1981.

As with heart transplants, it was not without controversy, as is made clear in this article from *World Medicine* in November 1984:

The first few British heart–lung operations, and the heart transplant recently performed on ten-day-old baby Hollie Roffey, mark equally adventurous though contrasting developments in cardiac transplantation over the past year. But the chronic shortage of donors remains, the Government has still to come up with enough cash, and professional and public doubts have been voiced about the worth of such surgery.

The morbid TV coverage that accompanied the initial heart–lung patient's agonised wait for a donor can have encouraged no one. Though the recent record gives hope, the first two heart–lung transplant recipients survived less than two weeks. And the operation on Hollie Roffey was surely premature.

It was inevitable that transplanting a baby's heart would arouse controversy. For all the early uncritical media coverage about glamorous medical advance, the chance of success was slim. And the view that the operation was pure research did not take long to surface.

Cardiac and heart–lung transplantation need steady progress, more money and more donors, not spectacular one-off operations. Earlier this year, the British Cardiac Society recommended the Government should allocate £2.5m to heart transplants. It estimated that 400–450 patients a year could benefit, mostly those suffering from end-stage ischaemic heart disease and cardiomyopathies with congestive heart failure. The health department is awaiting a report from Brunel University, which will show good rates of survival and greatly enhanced quality of life in the recipients of cardiac transplants. Despite this evidence, well publicised failures – even heroic ones – can only retard acceptance of the procedure.

At the moment, the heart–lung programme is a more logical development than extending heart transplants to very young patients. A heart–lung transplant is in some respects more straightforward than a cardiac implant.

Extracting the diseased organs from the recipient, and the healthy ones from the donor, takes longer, and obtaining a size match is more tricky, but the reconnection of the donor organs requires only three long sutures instead of four.

With a little luck and a lot of skill, implantation takes only half an hour.

Initial experience was discouraging. The first two operations took place at Harefield Hospital, in December 1983 and March 1984. Neither recipient survived more than two weeks. In the first case, the patient was too sick to stand much of a chance; in the second, the transplanted organs quickly failed, demonstrating the difficulty of selecting an appropriate donor.

Papworth transplanted two heart–lungs, in April and July 1984. Both patients were soon out of hospital.

Many of the technical problems have been overcome. As John Wallwork, consultant cardiothoracic surgeon at Papworth, says, 'The operation works. I have four people waiting, one of whom is very sick indeed. The reason we've only done two transplants so far is simply that we've had so few donors.'

On Friday 6 April 1984 *The Guardian* wrote:

Heart–lung swap patient is recovering
The British patient given a heart and lung transplant, Mrs Brenda Barber, aged 36, was recovering satisfactorily last night after an operation at Papworth Hospital, Cambridgeshire.

She was on a ventilator in the hospital's intensive care unit but had regained consciousness and had been visited by her husband, Mr Stephen Barber from Lewisham, south London.

Mrs Barber had suffered from a potentially lethal lung disease, but first reports suggested that her heart and other organs had suffered only minimal damage. If this is correct she should have substantially greater chance of surviving than the two patients given heart–lung transplants at Harefield Hospital who died because damage to other organs put too much strain on the new hearts.

Mrs Barber, who has a five year old daughter Samantha Jane, was given a new heart only because the combined operation is technically simpler – lung transplants have proved unsuccessful.

Mr Wallwork, it appears, intends to use the operation to treat patients with primary lung disease and heart conditions.

She was being treated at Brompton Hospital, London, when the body of a suitable donor arrived at Papworth on Wednesday. She was taken to Cambridgeshire and a 12-strong team began the operation at 1.18 am yesterday, finishing at 7.25 am.

Mr Edwards would not give details of the donor because he said the family did not want any publicity.

In 1989, ten years after the first heart transplant at Papworth, the *Sunday Times* wrote an article, with a photograph of Papworth's first heart–lung transplant patient, which summarised the progress that had been made in the ten years:

Five years ago Brenda Barber, a London housewife, was near death. A progressive illness had destroyed her ability to breathe and she was in hospital, hardly able to move a muscle.

She agreed to become the first patient to receive a new heart and lungs in a single operation at Papworth Hospital, near Cambridge, famous for its heart transplant programme.

Today, in one of the most convincing demonstrations of the power of such surgery, she enjoys life to the full. And Papworth, which is about to celebrate the tenth anniversary of the launch of its transplant programme, expects such operations to be provided routinely through-out the NHS within a few years.

Since January 1979, 370 patients have undergone transplant surgery there, and 260 are still alive. Alan Gay, the longest-surviving heart patient, had his opera-tion in July 1980. Barber, the longest survivor among a growing band of heart and lung patients, was operated on in April 1984.

Later this month, about 250 doctors and health man-agers will analyse the costs and benefits of transplant surgery as part of a two-day conference in Cambridge, held to mark the anniversary.

The Papworth team will present results of research showing that a majority of transplant patients experience a huge increase in the quality of life as well as an exten-sion of years.

That seems particularly true of the heart–lung group, and Barber still has not lost her delight at doing everyday tasks and being a mother again to her daughter Samantha, 10.

'People couldn't understand why I liked hoovering so much when I came out of hospital,' she said. 'But once you have been so close to death, you appreciate everything in life more.

'Samantha was three when I went into hospital. My illness was getting worse every week. I couldn't even move my legs without being out of breath.

'It was Samantha who kept me going while I was waiting for a suitable heart and lung. I kept thinking I must hang on so I could bring her up. The doctors told me I had a 50:50 chance with the operation. But I had nothing to lose because I knew I was dying anyway.

'The first thing I noticed when I woke was that I could breathe normally. Having gasped for every breath for two years, it was marvellous.'

The anniversary conference will be told by John Wallwork, director of Papworth's heart–lung transplant programme, that the operation has fully met expectations, though improvements are still sought: 77 per cent of patients are living for more than a year, and survival at three years is 53 per cent.

Recipients include growing numbers of young people with cystic fibrosis, an inherited disorder causing great suffering and an early death through over-production of mucus. Transplanted lungs do not carry the defective gene, and remain free of the disease.

The heart transplant programme, started by the surgeon Terence English, is offering even better chances:

with the latest combinations of anti-rejection drugs, nearly four out of five patients are living for three years, and more than three in five are still alive after five years.

The operations are of proven value, English says. 'I would like to see a lot more medical activities subjected to the same vigorous cost-benefit analysis we have undergone.'

Time in hospital has been cut from seven or eight weeks to two or three, with an extra week or two in village accommodation before the patient returns home. The cost is about £15,000 a patient in the first year, including drugs, and £3,000–£5,000 a year thereafter.

Problems remain. One is the supply of donor organs: the greater the success of transplants, the greater is the demand.

Until now, expansion has been achieved through multiple organ removal. But, overall, the pool of donors has remained steady recently.

Medical leaders argue that it could be increased if doctors made more effort to raise organ donation with relatives.

An outstanding contribution

When Professor John Wallwork retired in July 2011, at the age of 64, his achievements were honoured at a symposium at Robinson College, Cambridge. (Robinson College was appropriate in view of David Robinson's donation to Papworth Hospital in 1981 of £300,000 (£1.5 million in today's money) for the hospital to continue its heart and lung transplant research and development.)

Wallwork said:

I am proud of what we have achieved, especially the increasing survival rates after the operations.

What I will miss the most is the everyday comradeship with my colleagues. It is a very important hospital and it has been a privilege to be a part of it.

The Chief Executive of Papworth Hospital, Stephen Bridge, added:

John has made an outstanding contribution to heart and lung surgery and transplantation at Papworth, in the UK and across the world.

He leaves behind an impressive legacy in the transplant service at Papworth and has trained many overseas transplant surgeons who have subsequently set up transplant programmes in their own countries. It has been a pleasure to work with him and he will be missed greatly at Papworth.

Cambridge First published photographs of Wallwork, one showing him carrying out a heart and lung transplant, and wrote:

A Cambridge surgeon who has saved 3,000 lives and conducted the first heart and lung transplant in Europe ends his remarkable career next week.

A Cambridge surgeon who hit the headlines in 1984 after conducting Europe's first successful heart and lung transplant is retiring next week after granting thousands of patients the gift of life.

Professor John Wallwork leaves Papworth Hospital on July 8 after securing the specialist heart and lung hospital's place in history books and helping make it the country's main heart and lung transplant centre.

Together with Addenbrooke's surgeon Prof Sir Roy Calne, Prof Wallwork carried out the world's first heart, lung and liver transplant at Papworth in 1986.

At a time when he had a young family, Prof Wallwork and two other surgeons were available night and day, in the hope of receiving a call that would bring years of life to somebody awaiting an organ transplant.

And as organs tend to be harvested after a hospital's daily surgery list is complete, this meant working round the clock.

Prof Wallwork would wait for an organ and recipient to arrive at Papworth – often by helicopter onto the village's cricket pitch – so that transplant surgery could be undertaken as a matter of urgency and ideally within four hours of the donor being harvested.

He said: 'By their very nature transplant operations are impossible to plan because you don't know when an organ will become available.

'And you forget all this started before mobile phones were available.

'The 1980s were very exciting times as we were always developing new ideas and techniques.

'In the early years of transplantation all the patients were in the news but now you find they are going back and living normal lives.

'And it is good for them not being celebrities.

'The International Society for Heart and Lung Transplantation started in 1981, initially attended by a small number of delegates. There are now 2,000 delegates attending this prestigious meeting each year.'

Both Prof Wallwork and Sir Terence English, who carried out the first successful heart transplant at Papworth Hospital in 1979, are past presidents.

The longest surviving combined heart and lung transplant patient is cystic fibrosis sufferer Julie Bennett who Prof Wallwork operated on 26 years ago.

Like all transplant patients at Papworth, Ms Bennett has had regular appointments at the hospital ever since, despite having to travel from her home in Chepstow in the Welsh borders.

She said: 'When I had my transplant in 1985 it really was groundbreaking surgery and I never dreamt that I would be here 26 years later to see John Wallwork retire.

'I never thought that he would leave Papworth before I did.

'Words cannot describe the gratitude that I feel. He and the team at Papworth Hospital have really become like my second family.

'I will miss John immensely but I do wish him a long and happy retirement.'

Prof Wallwork said he, in turn, was surprised to be retiring while Papworth Hospital is still located in the village.

The specialist hospital is due to move onto the biomedical campus at the Addenbrooke's Hospital site in Cambridge in 2015.

Prof Wallwork reflected: 'When I came here they told me we would be moving within three years and it's nearly 30 years on now.

'I would like to see Papworth Hospital retain its ethos. Its name is important but it is the people who work in the hospital that make it special, for the patients of today and for the patients who will be treated in the new Papworth Hospital.'

More than 2,000 open heart surgery procedures are undertaken at Papworth Hospital each year and up to 100 heart and lung transplant operations are performed.

More than half the patients survive more than 10 years after transplant and have a marked improvement in their quality of life following surgery.

Prof Wallwork conducted his final operation earlier this month.

In addition to pioneering heart and lung transplant surgery, he has conducted research into why organs are rejected as well as undertaking trials into how animal organs can be genetically modified for human use.

He has also trained surgeons across the globe in addition to those in the UK.

When asked of his retirement plans, Prof Wallwork said he was keen to promote the planned research institute linked to the new hospital building where his legacy of research can be developed.

'Our health service can only provide up-to-date first class care if it is allowed also to be innovative which is why the institute is going to be so important' he said.

The *Hunts Post* added:

Wallwork began his training in Edinburgh and he would like to record his gratitude to Philip Caves, who, working closely with the ISHLT (International Society for Heart and Lung Transplantation) President, Margaret Billingham, developed the cardiac bioptome and endocardial biopsy technique. Access to tissue from the transplanted heart enabled the Stanford group to define cardiac rejection which later evolved into the ISHLT grading system.

After completing his surgical training in Edinburgh, Prof Wallwork trained with Prof Norman Shumway of Stanford University, California – dubbed the 'father of heart transplantation' – in the United States.

Chapter 6

MECHANICAL HEARTS

'Very well and wide awake'
An ethical alternative
Transfer of non-beating heart

'Very well and wide awake'

As we have seen, transplantation has been a driving force at Papworth and most of the other treatments have been developed thanks to Papworth's pioneering work in transplantation.

Cardiac and lung transplantation was a national service, funded centrally until 2014. However, a zonal retrieval system, driven by the national shortage of donor organs, has now been introduced. As a consequence Papworth now receives about 70 per cent of its new patients from just three of the eight health regions. The service carries out between 80 and 100 transplants per year. Referrals are accepted from all parts of the country, and suitable patients are admitted for a three- to four-day assessment period and subsequently may be accepted on to the waiting list. Following transplantation, patients spend on average 20 to 30 days in hospital. They return to Papworth for routine and emergency investigations and treatment for the rest of their lives.

However, there are cases where a donor organ cannot be found in time for transplantation, and Papworth now has an established programme for the use of mechanical devices led by the director of the transplant service, Steven Tsui. Many of the patients fitted with mechanical devices are well enough to go home while awaiting a transplant.

Back in the spring of 1994, *The Times* had written:

Surgeons set to carry out first artificial heart implant in UK
Britain's first artificial heart implant operation is likely to be carried out within the next few weeks.

Surgeons and medical staff at Papworth Hospital have almost completed their preparations for the operations after months of research and training.

The recipient of the artificial heart will be one of a group of seriously ill patients in imminent danger of dying because no suitable donor heart can be found.

The hospital has been given nine of the plastic devices by Humana Inc, the American-based international health-care organisation.

A spokesman for Papworth emphasised yesterday that the 10-ounce Jarvik-7 hearts will not be implanted per-manently. The intention is to replace them with donor organs as soon as possible.

The artificial heart has been given to patients in the USA in the past three years. Of three survivors, Mr William Schroeder, aged 52, has lived longest, passing the first anniversary of his operation last month.

Britain's first implant will be carried out at Papworth by Mr Terence English, who went to the Human Heart Institute In Louisville, Kentucky earlier this year to study the techniques.

A few weeks ago, nurses from the institute arrived at Papworth to help train nurses in caring for implant patients.

The Jarvik-7 is powered by a 323lb compressor at the patient's bedside but a portable compressor weighing about 11lb can be used to give mobility. [...]

Although Papworth has been given nine artificial hearts the hospital is unlikely to use them all within the next year and each is likely to be used more than once.

The operation will be restricted to a small number of patients because of the availability of donor hearts and the much higher cost of nursing artificial heart patients.

And on 27 August 1994 *The Times* wrote, under the heading, 'Patient "very well and wide awake"' and 'Surgeons give patient first artificial heart':

A 62-year-old man has been given an artificial heart in a pioneering operation at Papworth Hospital in Cambridgeshire.

The £40,000 metal and plastic device, the size of a bag of sugar and weighing 1½lb, will stay in his body for the rest of his life or for as long as the device lasts. Unlike earlier artificial hearts, it is not intended simply to keep him alive until a transplant heart becomes available.

The device does not replace the natural heart but helps it to carry out its most demanding function, pumping blood around the body. The patient, who has not been named, received the device in a four hour operation on Thursday.

The operating team was led by the transplant surgeon, John Wallwork, who said yesterday that the patient 'is very well, wide awake and in very good shape'. If all goes well, he will return home in due course, leading a virtually normal life.

Up to 20 more patients could be given the artificial hearts at Papworth over the next three years in the first clinical trials designed to assess their effectiveness as permanent implants.

The manufacturer, Baxter Novacor, said that it has used the devices in test programmes for up to three years without failure. Some 250 have been implanted, mostly in the United States, for patients waiting to have transplants, but Papworth's is the first meant for permanent use.

The artificial heart, known as a Left Ventricular Assist Device, reinforces the pumping action of the left ventricle, which as the hardest-working part is most likely to deteriorate in cases of heart failure. Electric power comes from batteries worn on a belt around the waist and connected through the skin. The device keeps pace with the patient's natural heart through the control of a tiny microprocessor on the belt, with the two battery packs weighing a total of 6½lb.

The operation is the first in a trial planned by the hospital to assess the clinical effectiveness of the device. Eight patients will be chosen for a pilot study and divided into two groups, half having the device implanted and the other half continuing on normal medication. Their progress will be compared over two years.

Mr Wallwork said: 'The purpose of this trial is to evaluate the assist device as a permanent implant for patients with established irreversible cardiac failure.'

He added: 'If it proves to be successful, the next question is, is this device as good as a transplant? Artificial devices have problems in the same way as transplant organs. At this stage, it is too early to say what the outcome will be.'

Julian Smith, a senior surgical registrar who took part in the operation, said: 'It is a world first because this has been put in with the intent of the device being used as a permanent implant for an end-stage heart failure patient. Previously the intention has been to transplant, but some patients are not suitable for this.'

The demand is potentially great. American scientists have estimated that between 70,000 and 140,000 people worldwide could benefit. The device would give hope to patients who are too old for a transplant and in any case supplies of donor hearts are never likely to be sufficient. An alternative is to use hearts from pigs genetically engineered so that they are not rejected by the body, a programme in which Papworth has played a leading part. But the first test of this lies several years ahead.

The man who developed the artificial heart, Dr Peer Portner of the American Baxter Health Care Corporation, has spent 25 years refining the technology. The safety record of such devices is good. Another company that makes them, Thermo Cardiosystems, of Woburn, Massachusetts, said there had been only one death from mechanical failure. Experience has also reduced the danger of blood clots forming.

One potential drawback is that the cable from the batteries penetrates the skin, which could be a source of infection. Future devices will avoid this by placing electrical coils inside and outside the skin.

The costs of the operation and the pilot study of eight patients will be paid by Papworth Hospital from charitable donations. For a full trial involving 40 patients, additional funding will be needed.

The hospital, near Cambridge, has been the leader in organ transplantation for more than 15 years. Since

January 1979, when the first transplant was carried out there, more than 500 patients have been given new organs.

An ethical alternative

The Times also wrote this leading article:

THE HEART OF THE MATTER

Mechanical devices are an ethical alternative to live organs

The revolutionary operation performed at Papworth Hospital this week may well open a new era in heart surgery. For the first time a patient who would not previously have been able to survive without a complete heart transplant has been equipped with a permanent mechanical left ventricle – not a 'mechanical heart' as has been said misleadingly by some. But the dramatic implications are no less for that: the success of this technique could mean that fewer full transplant operations will be necessary.

Transplants have never been a complete answer to heart failure. Not all patients are suitable and those who are must take anti-rejection drugs for the rest of their lives. But the most serious shortcoming of transplant surgery is that it relies on a steady supply of donor organs – creating both technical and ethical problems.

The short 'lifespan' of usable vital organs means that they must be removed from the deceased with little delay. Since healthy organs are required, those most likely to be used belong to the young and fit: usually victims of accidental death. Thus families have to be asked to agree to an organ donation when they are shocked by an unexpected bereavement. Many medical personnel have conscientious objections even to broaching such a request at a time when they feel that their first duty is to deal with personal grief and trauma. The premium on accidental deaths also means that every improvement in public safety – such as car seatbelts – exacerbates the dearth of available organs.

One solution to the scarcity of human organs has been thought to lie in the use of animal organs. One of the surgeons who led this week's surgical breakthrough, Dr John Wallwork, has been known as an advocate of the use of animal tissue in transplant surgery. Animal parts such as heart valves have proved serviceable in human treatment. But the use of whole animal organs has so far never been successful. The only solution lay with genetic engineering: the implanting of human genes into animals whose organs were close to those of humans, thus producing genetically manipulated species whose DNA composition would be more compatible with the human body.

Mice, sheep and pigs are now being bred with human genetic components for medical purposes. This may offer a way out of the human donor problem but it also has moral implications. There may seem to be little differ-ence between breeding animals for food and breeding them for transplant. But animals devouring one another is part of the natural order of things: interfering in the genetic make-up of a species has a metaphysical con-notation which is far more hubristic. By inventing a mechanical device to replace the pumping action of the heart, medical science may finally have produced a breakthrough which actually reduces our ethical qualms instead of adding to them.

Steven Tsui has been a consultant surgeon at Papworth since 1998 and although he's clinical director of transplant surgery, he spends much of his time doing what he calls his 'day job' of routine heart operations.

He admits that he'd always been intrigued by the concept of a totally artificial heart. In fact the only reason he hadn't attempted the operation before was because the machines, or 'drive consoles', needed to power artificial hearts were so big: 'They are about the size of a large refrigerator, and weigh about 400lb, so you can imagine that, while the patient may be kept alive, they don't have much in the way of quality of life.

'They're imprisoned in their environment, and I didn't really think that just keeping people alive artificially like that was an appropriate thing to do.'

When he discovered that an American company, SynCardia, were developing a portable drive console which the patient could easily carry around, he decided immediately that this was something Papworth should offer.

It took two years to get the go-ahead, and by January 2011 funding was approved. Steven and a team of medics headed to Paris to train for the operation, and by April everything was ready to go. But who would be the first patient?

This is what the *Cambridge Evening News* wrote on 1 September 2011:

Matthew Green was dying. Desperate for a heart transplant, the 40-year-old had been on Papworth's waiting list for a donor heart for many months but, with no suitable match on the horizon, his time was running out.

But luck was on Matthew's side and, thanks to a revolutionary new piece of equipment, earlier this summer he was fitted with a completely artificial heart by cardiothoracic surgeon Mr Steven Tsui.

Not surprisingly, the pair hit the headlines when Matthew was well enough to face the press last month. But what few people knew was that, had it not been for a chance glimpse of a TV programme more than 30 years ago, Steven might never have become a surgeon.

The year was 1979 and Steven, who's originally from Hong Kong, was studying for his O-levels at a Berkshire boarding school when the UK's very first successful heart transplant was carried out.

'I didn't normally watch telly, but that day I remember walking past the television room and seeing it on the news. And I was mesmerised,' he recalls.

'I thought to myself "that sounds really cool, that's what I want to do", and I went to see my schoolteachers about it.'

It was in September last year that Matthew Green first came to Papworth with arrhythmogenic right ventricular cardiomyopathia (ARVC), a heart muscle disease which can result in heart failure and sudden death.

Matthew's condition had deteriorated to the point where a heart transplant was his only hope, but his outlook wasn't bright.

'He's actually a very big chap: he's about 6ft 4in,' explains Steven.

'You can't put a Mini engine into a truck and expect it to work, so for a big person, you need to have a big donor. Paradoxically, you can put a big engine into a small car and it will work, so big donor hearts are in huge demand.'

Not only that, but Matthew has blood group O, which means that he can only receive an organ from a blood group O donor: 'Whereas if you're a blood group O donor, you are a universal donor. So a large blood group O donor heart is very hard to come by, because you can put it into pretty much any recipient and it will work.'

Matthew languished on the waiting list, and his health began to fade. 'By April he was in very bad shape,' recalls Steven. 'He couldn't pump enough blood around the body to keep the vital organs working properly, so his liver function was deteriorating, his kidney function was deteriorating, and he was basically dying from his heart failure.

'He was running out of time. And knowing that we were not going to find a suitable donor heart for him very quickly, that's when we started thinking well, maybe this is the right thing for him.'

Steven and the team then discussed the idea with Matthew: 'Initially I think the family was more horrified than he was. The concept of actually taking away your heart, and putting an artificial heart inside you, was a foreign concept for them.

'But for Matthew, I think deep down he knew that it was his only chance and he very quickly made the decision that this was the right thing for him.'

The operation was scheduled for June 9, 'and you can imagine that even though I've done thousands of heart operations, I kept on rehearsing the steps in my head beforehand,' admits Steven.

Happily the procedure went smoothly, and as soon as Matthew was wheeled out of theatre, people commented on how wonderfully pink he looked: 'Before he was blue and grey and very sick-looking, so as soon as the pump went in and the heart was working, he had life in him.'

For Matthew, his new heart has given him a new lease of life – but it's only a temporary measure: artificial hearts can never replace transplanting a real human heart, as they will always need a source of power: 'You still need to have a cable that comes out of the body and is plugged into a controller, and that means there are limitations in term of what you can do,' explains Steven.

'You can't go swimming, you can't soak in a bath, and the patients have to carry a spare battery around. When my mobile phone runs out of battery it's kind of irritating, but when their pump runs out of battery it's life or death. So it's a psychological burden.

'If there's no donor heart it's going to be a life-saver, but the quality of life is not as good. We have done over a thousand heart transplants, and we have patients who do very remarkable things, like running the London Marathon and all sorts of things that you can't really dream of doing with an artificial blood pump. So heart transplantation is still the gold standard.'

It's thanks to surgeons like Steven that people continue to flourish with their new hearts, which is the reason, he says, that he loves his job.

'We hope that we can make a positive difference in people's lives. And whilst every one of our patients is precious, with them there are families and friends, so what we do to that one person – improving their quality of life and their life expectancy – actually has a major impact on everybody around them.

'Without this treatment Matthew's wife may not have a husband anymore, and Matthew's son may not have a father anymore.

'So even after a lot of blood and sweat and sleepless nights and anguish and worry, eventually when we deliver the patient back to their family, it's extremely rewarding.'

The heart surgeon Stephen Large wrote in 2015:

The Demand for Heart Transplantation
Despite advances in mechanical support, heart transplantation still remains the gold standard treatment for end stage drug resistant heart failure. It provides both excellent long-term survival and a near normal quality of life. Unfortunately as the number of patients eligible for heart transplantation continues to rise, the number of suitable donors after brain death (DBD) continues to fall. In the United Kingdom this increasing disparity between

demand and supply results in less than half of patients being transplanted whilst 43 per cent of the waiting list are either permanently removed or die waiting for a heart transplant.

With the heart transplant waiting list increasing at an exponential rate, attention has fallen on extended criteria donors (ECD). In Europe, it is now routine to consider those hearts from donors up to 65 years old, those with ventricular hypertrophy or those with a history of prolonged cardiac arrest. However, even after incorporating these marginal donors, there remains an increasing shortfall in meeting demand. In an attempt to push the boundaries still further, some enthusiasts are looking toward the Donation after Circulatory Determined Death (DCD) donor to bridge the gap. DCD donors are patients who have sustained catastrophic brain injury but who will not proceed to brain stem death or where brain stem testing would be inappropriate. After consultation between the intensive care doctors and the family, a decision to withdraw therapy is made after it has been established that it would be futile to continue and not in the best interests of the patient.

Transfer of non-beating heart
In spring 2015 the *Cambridge News* wrote:

The first 'dead' heart transplant in Europe has been carried out in the UK. The procedure involves taking a heart that had not been beating for some time, and making it work inside the body of a living recipient.

This is markedly different from normal transplants, which involve the beating heart of a living person who has been declared brainstem dead. In this reverse case, the heart came from a victim of circulatory death – their other organs gave out. The new approach involves restoring function to a dead heart, before placing it into an Organ Care System (OCS) to maintain quality before surgery.

The recipient was 60 year-old Huseyin Ulucan, from London. The Papworth hospital in Cambridgeshire, where the still revolutionary procedure was performed, said he's making 'remarkable progress' at home, after just four days in intensive care, following the transplant.

The hospital is also optimistic about the future: success in this field means 25 per cent more hearts to work with in the future, and thus, more lives saved. This amounts to hundreds of people in the UK alone.

'Using techniques developed to recover the abdominal organs in non-heart beating donors, we wanted to apply similar techniques to hearts from these donors,' said Simon Messer, cardiothoracic transplant registrar.

'Until this point we were only able to transplant organs from DBD (donation after brain-stem death) donors. However, research conducted at Papworth allowed us to develop a new technique not used anywhere else in the world to ensure the best possible outcome for our patients using hearts from non-beating heart donors.'

Last year, Australian doctors announced the world's first successful 'dead' heart transplant, using a machine to reanimate and test the organ before deciding to use it.

By contrast the British team used a pump to restart the heart in the donor body, allowing its performance to be monitored as blood flowed around for almost an hour. It was then transported using the usual 'heart in a box' device to keep the organ nourished.

Stephen Large, with his junior colleagues including Simon Messer, whose research paved the way for the transplant, estimates that 50 extra hearts a year could be transplanted from donors previously considered unsuitable. About 170 patients a year are given heart transplants and there are 257 people on the waiting list. One in ten dies waiting.

The new method will continue to be tested with the hope of making it standard across the NHS.

Steven Tsui, clinical director of transplantation at Papworth, said: 'We are delighted by Mr Ulucan's progress.'

Professor James Neuberger, head of organ donation at NHS Blood and Transplant, said: 'We hope Papworth's work and similar work being developed elsewhere will result in more hearts being donated and more patients benefiting from a transplant in the future.'

Mr Ulucan, the recipient, had had considerable difficulty leading a normal life since 2008, when he'd had a heart attack.

'Before the surgery, I could barely walk and I got out of breath very easily, I really had no quality of life,' he told the BBC this week.

'Now I'm feeling stronger every day, and I walked into the hospital this morning without any problem.'

Stephen Large, the surgeon who led the operation, said: 'This is a very exciting development. By enabling the safe use of this kind of donor heart, we could significantly increase the total number of heart transplants each year, saving hundreds of lives.'

Why was this technique not widely used before? To answer this question we need to look at the background to DCD transplantation.

It was almost 50 years since the world's first successful heart transplant. Considering the controversies surrounding DCD heart transplantation it is somewhat ironic that Christiaan Barnard transplanted the first clinical heart from a DCD donor. Success was dependent upon a myocardial preservation strategy that relied on prompt reperfusion within the donor, hypothermia and continuous perfusion during implantation, so minimising ischaemia. As brain stem testing became established following the Harvard Criteria, hearts no longer had to endure the obligatory warm ischaemic period associated with DCD donation. The elaborate methods of myocardial preservation soon became redundant in favour of the simplistic attraction of cold storage of the DBD donor heart.

Today, nearly half a century later, desperation has once again led to the DCD donor. This is a direction abdominal transplant surgeons turned to almost ten years ago, as they were also faced with falling numbers of DBD donors and relatively little to lose. Within the UK, DCD donation for liver and kidney transplantation is well established. Over the last decade, DCD donation has increased from 1.1 to

7.9 donors per million population. DCD renal transplantation has been the major stakeholder, with DCD kidney donation increasing seven-fold. The DCD liver donor now forms 25 per cent of the national liver transplant service. Although DCD lung transplantation is still regarded as relatively novel, outcomes have been shown to be equivalent to the DBD programme.

Forecasts for DCD heart transplantation predict that if adopted, overall heart transplant activity would increase by 20 per cent. These conservative forecasts model on donors less than 50 years old, on no inotropic support and withdrawal to perfusion times of less than 30 minutes. In the future these strict criteria will probably be relaxed to some extent, allowing access to greater donor numbers.

Although both a need and a potential for DCD heart transplantation have been identified, significant obstacles exist before a successful programme can be implemented in today's society. Although there have been several successful DCD human heart transplants performed in the past, they have all evolved strategies to reduce the ischaemic burden.

In order to establish a successful, universal clinical DCD heart programme, current ethical boundaries must be recognised and accepted, and strategies evolved to recondition and assess DCD hearts prior to transplantation. If careful assessment and selection of the DCD heart is disregarded, simply relying on familiar techniques of cold storage, a programme of DCD donor heart transplantation will undoubtedly end in failure.

Over the last 50 years of heart transplantation little investment has been made in donor heart reconditioning, preservation or functional assessment. This has inhibited progress in the development of a DCD heart transplant programme and discouraged surgeons from pursuing the four DBD hearts currently declined on grounds of poor function or coronary disease for each donor heart currently accepted. So what is the situation today? Isolated perfusion of the donor heart is now possible with the TransMedics Organ Care System (OCS), the only commercial available continuous ex vivo perfusion platform. This was originally designed to offer functional assessment but later modified to offer simpler, safer donor heart root perfusion after the complexities of managing the working heart in the clinical field were realised.

In summary, surgeons are faced with a growing demand for heart transplantation in the face of declining donor heart numbers. The possibility of increasing the donor pool further by accessing the DCD donor is very welcome. Unfortunately, in order to accomplish this potential 20 per cent increase in heart transplant activity, investment is required in machine perfusion, assessment and optimisation of perfusate. This investment may be wisely spent, as successful DCD heart recovery may translate into improving those numerous DBD hearts rejected on grounds of poor function. This all has great promise for the future of heart transplantation.

Ben Milstein performed the first open-heart surgery at Papworth in 1958 and became a father figure known for his wise counsel and forthright attitude.

Christopher Parish.

Keith Castle celebrating the success of his heart transplantation.

Hugh Fleming was the first cardiologist to be appointed in East Anglia.

Sir Terence English in front of the pond and Papworth Hall on 3 July 1998.

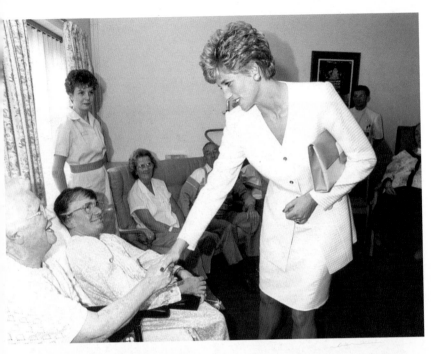

HRH Diana, Princess of Wales on a visit to Papworth, 17 June 1993.

Professor Tim Higenbottam established the prostacyclin service.

Professor Sir Roy Calne performed the first liver transplantation in Europe in 1968.

Dr John Shneerson developed the Respiratory Support and Sleep Centre (RSSC) at Papworth.

Dr Chris Flower pushed the boundaries of radiology, pioneering new techniques.

Celia Hyde, a senior nurse who became the first modern Matron at Papworth.

David Stone became Medical Director at Papworth from 2002 to 2009.

John Wallwork in front of the pond and Princess Ward, Papworth, on 3 July 1998.

Sir Terence English, Professor Norman Shumway, Sir Magdi Yacoub and John Wallwork at Papworth on 3 July 1998 on the occasion of the official opening of the new transplant building.

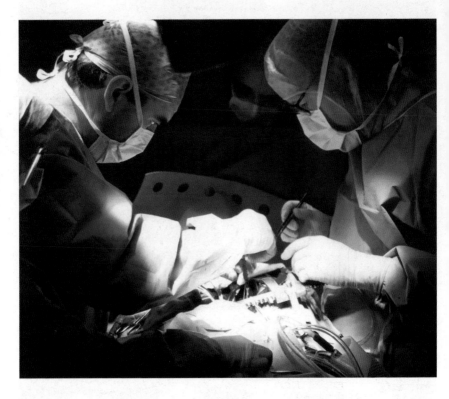

An operation.

The Cardiac Block viewed from across the pond.

Mr Francis Wells, a consultant cardiothoracic surgeon at Papworth, specialises in mitral valve reconstruction, aortic valve repair and surgery of the aorta.

John Wallwork (right) with Keith McNeil, an internationally recognised expert in lung transplantation and pulmonary vascular disease who left Papworth to become CEO of Cambridge University Hospitals.

Susan Stewart was Medical Director from 2009 to 2015 after 20 years of specialising in pathology.

Stephen Bridge with Audrey Stenner, Chairman of Papworth NHS Trust.

The Duchess of Gloucester meeting the theatre staff at Papworth.

A long-living guardian.

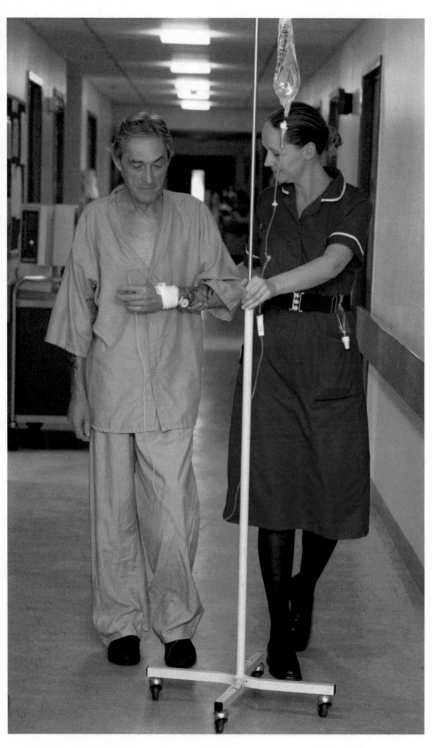

Nursing care.

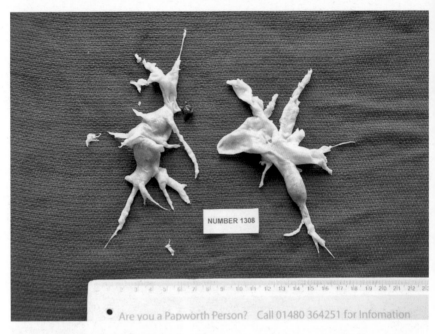

NUMBER 1308

Thromboendarterectomy specimen.

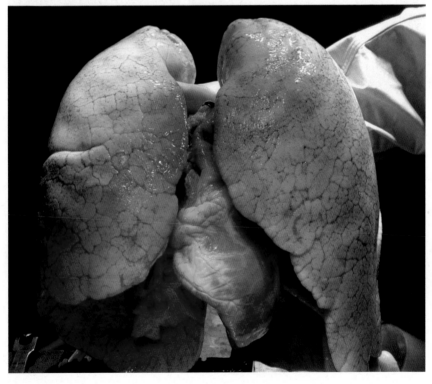

The heart of the matter.

Chapter 7

PAPWORTH'S RANGE OF TREATMENTS

Papworth's services
Cardiology
Radiology and Pathology
Cardiac surgery
TAVI
Measuring outcomes
Chest medicine
RSSC
TCCA
Thoracic surgery
CT scanner

Papworth's services

Papworth Hospital is the UK's largest specialist cardio-thoracic hospital and the country's main heart and lung transplant centre, treating over 25,000 in-patient and day cases and over 75,000 out-patients each year from across the UK. Its services are internationally recognised and include cardiology, respiratory medicine and cardiothoracic surgery and transplantation.

But there is a danger that heart transplants, important though they are, capture the headlines so that all the other treatments and successes of Papworth Hospital are lost, even though many of them have been developed because of Papworth's success with transplants.

The reality is that the Papworth Trust employs more than 1,800 people across a wide range of staff groups including doctors, nurses, cardiac surgeons, cardiologists, cardiac physiologists, thoracic surgeons, respiratory physicians, specialist cardiothoracic anaesthetists, intensive care specialists, radiologists, pathologists, dieticians, speech therapists, physiotherapists, pharmacists, clinical educators, the infection control team, and the administrative and clerical staff.

The hospital's facilities include five operating theatres and five angiographic suites as well as 290 beds, spread over a dozen wards and units, and including a recently extended Clinical Care Area.

Papworth Hospital is one of the UK's leading centres in coronary angiography, angioplasty and stenting, and for intervention in structural heart disease including closure of septal defects; for transcatheter treatment of valve disease;

for electrophysiology (EP); for device implantation; for coronary artery bypass grafting (CABG); and for valve repair or replacement.

Cardiology

Hugh Fleming, in a report dated May 1972, noted:

> The management of common cardiac conditions, in particular angina, heart failure and acute myocardial infarction, using primarily non-invasive techniques, was carried out within local acute hospitals. The only invasive cardiological procedure that was commonly employed outside specialist cardiothoracic facilities was cardiac pacing. The pacing service, partly domiciliary and partly in peripheral clinics, was provided by consultant cardiologists for patients requiring this procedure in East Anglia. A hub and spoke arrangement for the deployment of consultant cardiologists had been in place for several years. Of the thirteen consultant cardiologists who treated patients at Papworth, only five were based at the trust; seven were employed by local acute trusts, and one specialist attended from St George's, London. All had sessions at Papworth. Consultant out-patient clinics were held around the region at the following hospitals: Addenbrooke's Hospital, Cambridge, Newmarket Hospital, West Suffolk Hospital, Ipswich Hospital, Hinchingbrooke Hospital, Bedford Hospital, Peterborough District Hospital, Queen Elizabeth Hospital, King's Lynn, James Paget Hospital, Great Yarmouth, Saffron Walden Community Hospital and Norfolk and Norwich Hospital.

Angiography

Patients who required angiography were then admitted to Papworth, with the exception of those who were cared for by cardiologists based at the Norfolk and Norwich Hospital. The distances involved in travelling to Papworth made the provision of an angiographic service in Norwich both effective and efficient.

An extensive array of non-invasive investigations and expertise was available at Papworth. There was an echocardiographic department with Doppler and transoesophageal facilities, and a nuclear department with a new gamma camera and facilities for chromographic and dynamic imaging. There were also facilities for electrophysiological study and catheter ablation. Invasive studies were carried out in two angiography laboratories where investigations such as cardiac catheterisation, percutaneous transluminal angioplasty (PTCA), coronary stenting and balloon valvuloplasty were performed. Other techniques in development included percutaneous myocardial revascularisation and atherectomy.

Angiography is best carried out in a specialist cardiothoracic facility where patients might proceed at the same time to PTCA or where complications require that the patient is prepared for immediate CABG. Nevertheless, issues of accessibility might dictate that local acute hospitals far from specialist facilities should establish angiographic facilities. In recent years cardiologists at the Norfolk and Norwich have safely provided such a service for their patients, and, provided the number of procedures at other local hospitals allow the appropriate level of expertise to be maintained, this trend could be extended elsewhere, particularly if there were only to be a single specialist cardiothoracic facility in the Region. At present, it is generally accepted that other invasive procedures such as PTCA should be carried out only at specialist facilities. Some patients with acute myocardial infarction will benefit from immediate angiography and PTCA. However, clinical opinion in the UK is probably of the view that the huge costs involved in establishing a 24-hour angiographic service in local acute hospitals to respond to this need is not justified by the marginal benefit gained over existing management strategies.

This primary angioplasty service is now established as the preferred treatment for acute heart attacks. Dr Sarah Clarke, who was Clinical Director of Cardiac Services from 2006 to 2012, developed and implemented the Primary Angioplasty Service for heart patients at Papworth. Dr Clarke is now President of the British Cardiovascular Society.

Arrhythmia

Papworth Hospital also leads the way in developments in cardiac arrhythmia.

Arrhythmias – problems with the heartbeat's rate or rhythm, where the hearts beats too quickly, too slowly or with an irregular rhythm – are thought to affect over one million people in the UK, and are one of the top ten reasons why people go to hospital.

Arrhythmias can disrupt the heart's ability to pump enough blood to the body, resulting in a lack of blood flow which can damage the brain, heart and other organs.

Papworth Hospital consultant cardiologist, Dr Andrew Grace, described by *The Lancet* as 'one of the world's leading heart rhythm specialists', is the lead author of a new *Lancet* series exploring the latest developments in the diagnosis, treatment and biology of cardiac arrhythmias.

He said in spring 2015:

> The progress in cardiology in general in the last twenty years has been remarkable and today cardiac electrophysiology, which not so long ago was essentially diagnostic, is now often curative. The current landscape in arrhythmia management would be unrecognisable to practitioners twenty years ago.
>
> Although we have made massive strides both in our understanding and treatment of arrhythmias, there are still gaps. For example, drug treatment remains an issue: the drugs are variably effective and do have side effects.

Dr Grace said he had seen the risk profile of his patients changing, with the increasing numbers experiencing atrial fibrillation only partly explained by ageing. Accordingly, a current focus of his research is on the metabolic basis of arrhythmia. He said:

> Obesity, diabetes and hypertension need to be controlled if we want to curb this growth. Looking to the future I see both opportunities and challenges ahead. Arrhythmia management has been transformed by the application of technology but to provide effective therapy for all our patients we will need to work harder to understand mechanisms.

A *Lancet* editorial accompanying the series concluded that:

> With the expected rapid advances in understanding
> and further translation of molecular evidence, better
> treatment of cardiac arrhythmias and higher rates of
> prevention of sudden cardiac death are likely in the not
> too distant future.

Cardiac imaging

Papworth's cardiology services are split into four areas: cardiac intensive care, cardiac rhythm management, structural cardiology and cardiac imaging. Cardiac imaging techniques include coronary catheterisation, echocardiogram, and intravascular ultrasound.

Coronary catheterisation uses pressure monitoring and blood sampling through a catheter inserted into the heart through blood vessels in the leg to determine the functioning of the heart, and, following injections of radiocontrast dye, uses X-ray fluoroscopy, typically at 30 frames per second, to visualise the position and volume of blood within the heart chambers and arteries. Coronary angiography is used to determine the patency and configuration of the coronary artery lumens.

Transthoracic echocardiogram uses ultrasonic waves for continuous heart chamber and blood movement visualisation. In recent times, it has become one of the most commonly used tools in diagnosis of heart problems, as it allows non-invasive visualisation of the heart and the blood flow through the heart, using a technique known as Doppler.

Transoesophageal echocardiogram (TOE) uses a specialised probe containing an ultrasound transducer at its tip, which is passed into the patient's oesophagus. It is used in diagnosis of various thoracic defects or damage, i.e. heart and lung imaging. It has some advantages and disadvantages over thoracic or intravascular ultrasound.

Intravascular ultrasound, also known as a percutaneous echocardiogram, is an imaging methodology using specially designed, long, thin, complex manufactured catheters attached to computerised ultrasound equipment to visualise the lumen and the interior wall of blood vessels.

Positron emission tomography (PET) is an imaging methodology for positron-emitting radioisotopes. PET enables visual image analysis of multiple different metabolic chemical processes and is thus one of the most flexible imaging technologies. Cardiology uses are growing very slowly due to technical and relative cost difficulties. Most uses are for research, not clinical purposes. Appropriate radioisotopes of elements within chemical compounds of the metabolic pathway being examined are used to make the location of the chemical compounds of interest visible in a PET scanner-constructed image.

Computed tomography angiography (CTA) is an imaging methodology using a ring-shaped machine with an X-ray source spinning around the circular path so as to bathe the inner circle with a uniform and known X-ray density. Cardiology uses are growing with the incredible developments in CT technology. Currently, multidetector CT, especially the 64 detector CT, is allowing cardiac studies to be made in just a few seconds (less than ten seconds, depending on the equipment and protocol used). These images are reconstructed using algorithms and software. Great development and growth will be seen in the short term, allowing radiologists to diagnose cardiac artery disease without anaesthesia and in a non-invasive way.

Magnetic resonance imaging (originally called nuclear magnetic resonance imaging) is an imaging methodology based on aligning the spin axis of nuclei within molecules of the object being visualised using both powerful superconducting magnets and radio frequency signals and detectors. Cardiology uses are growing, especially since MRI differentiates soft tissues better than CT and allows for comprehensive examinations including the quantitative assessment of size, morphology, function, and tissue characteristics in one single session. Current implementations for cardiology uses are sometimes limited by lengthy protocols, claustrophobia and contraindications based on some complex metallic implants (pacemakers, defibrillators, insulin pumps), while artificial valves and coronary stents are generally not problematic. Image quality can be reduced by the continuous movement of heart structures. There is a promising future in cardiac MRI by more efficient scans, increasing availability of scanners and more widespread knowledge about its clinical application.

Radiology and Pathology

Radiology is a medical specialty that uses imaging to diagnose and treat disease seen within the body. A variety of imaging techniques has been developed and now includes radiography, ultrasound, computed tomography (CT), positron emission tomography (PET) and magnetic resonance imaging (MRI) to diagnose or treat diseases.

Papworth has a full range of diagnostic facilities in its Radiology department, including CT scanning and nuclear medicine, but does not have MRI. It is staffed by four consultant radiologists. The Pathology department is staffed by three consultant histopathologists and houses the Public Health Laboratory Service microbiology service with a full-time consultant microbiologist. An immunopathology service started in 1995 with emphasis on providing a service in specialised areas such as transplantation and immuno-deficiency. General pathology services are provided from Hinchingbrooke Hospital and more specialised pathology from Addenbrooke's.

Cardiac surgery

Papworth Hospital is one of the UK's leading and largest specialist providers of cardiac surgery, after expansion in this area in the 1970s and 80s, including coronary artery bypass grafting, and the UK's largest valve repair/replacement centre. The hospital performs more major heart operations than any other single unit in the UK (around 2,400 per year).

The mainstay of cardiac surgery is coronary artery bypass grafting. This, together with surgery for valvular heart disease and a small number of other procedures, comprises the total number of operations requiring cardio-pulmonary bypass (pumps). The number of pumps carried out at Papworth has doubled in the past ten years. A regular audit is well established and reviews the procedures performed and their outcome over the following 30 days. Papworth contributes detailed activity data to the UK Cardiac Surgical Register on an annual basis. The hospital has a mortality rate (deaths within 30 days of operation) of less than 2 per cent, which is below that reported by the UK Register and compares favourably with other international centres of excellence.

All types of heart surgery in adults are available at Papworth, including the following:

Heart bypass (coronary artery bypass graft) operation. The main purpose of the operation is to relieve angina, especially if other less invasive methods are not suitable. Angina is a feeling of discomfort or pressure, usually felt in the middle of the chest, but sometimes in the arms, back, neck or jaw. It is an unpleasant feeling that occurs during exercise and goes away with rest. Because angina occurs on exertion, it can worsen a person's quality of life, limiting what they can do and enjoy.

The other purpose of the operation is to cut down the risk of heart attacks in the future. In some patients, the narrowing and blockages of arteries in the heart make heart attacks more likely. Some patients may consider having a heart bypass operation to reduce the risk of heart attack, even if they do not have troublesome angina, and for some people it may be possible to open up a coronary artery using a different surgical technique known as angioplasty, rather than a bypass.

This is a big operation. Usually the chest, back, neck, shoulders and legs can hurt, but this is easily treated with standard painkillers. The operation also makes patients feel tired and lacking in energy for the first few weeks.

Usually, angina disappears completely immediately after the operation and stays away for years. In many patients the risk of heart attack is also much less once they have recovered from the operation. The operation is done under general anaesthetic. The anaesthetist puts in many tubes and drips to monitor the patient and to give medicines. The chest is cut over the breastbone. The surgeon then takes a vein, usually from the leg, or artery, usually from inside the chest, and uses it to create a bypass around the blockage in the coronary artery. More than one bypass may be done, depending on how many block-ages there are. Often a heart–lung machine is used to keep the blood circulating while the heart is stopped for sur-gery. Sometimes it is possible to do the operation, without a machine, on the beating heart. When the bypasses are done, the heart is restarted, the machine stopped and the wounds are closed.

Aortic valve replacement is an operation in which a nar-rowed or leaky aortic valve is replaced by a valve made out of tissue or artificial material to relieve breathlessness and to help prevent heart failure. Papworth offers all types of aortic valve replacement as well as TAVI (transcatheter aortic valve implantation – see below).

Mitral valve surgery is an operation to repair or replace a narrowed or leaky mitral valve to relieve breathlessness and to help prevent heart failure. Papworth offers both approaches and has the largest number of successful mitral valve repair operations in the UK.

Blood flows from the lungs and enters the left atrium of the heart. The blood then flows into the left ventricle. The mitral valve is located between these two chambers. It makes sure that the blood keeps moving forward.

The results of mitral valve repair are excellent. For best results the patient should choose to have surgery at a centre that does many of these procedures. Papworth is a major centre for mitral repair, led by Francis Wells.

The patient will need a new valve if there is too much damage to the existing mitral valve. The surgeon will remove the mitral valve and sew a new one into place. There are two main types of new valves. Mechanical valves – of man-made materials, such as titanium and carbon – last the longest. The patient here will need to take blood-thinning medicine such as warfarin or aspirin, for the rest of their life. Biological valves are made of human or animal tissue. These valves last for ten to twelve years, but the patient may not need to take blood-thinners for the rest of their life.

The patient may need surgery if the mitral valve does not work properly because:

- The patient has mitral regurgitation – a mitral valve that does not close all the way and allows blood to leak back into the left atrium.
- The patient has mitral stenosis – a mitral valve that does not open fully and restricts blood flow.
- The valve has developed an infection (infectious endocarditis).

- The patient has severe mitral valve prolapse that is not controlled with medicine.

If the surgeon can repair the mitral valve, the patient may have ring annuloplasty. The surgeon repairs the ring-like part around the valve by sewing a ring of metal, cloth or tissue around the valve. For valve repair, the surgeon trims, shapes, or rebuilds one or both of the flaps that open and close the valve.

This is what Francis Wells said about the treatment of diseases of the mitral valve:

> The development of surgical treatment for diseases of the mitral and aortic valves is indeed a fascinating story, since it heralds the development of a whole new area of surgery – the ability to operate on the heart. Indeed many of the techniques used routinely in cardiac surgery have been developed as a result of interest in this field, and certainly, without the technological advances which have been made in the areas of cardiopulmonary bypass, implantable bioprosthetic materials, cardiac anaesthesia and post-operative care, there would be no story to tell.

Papworth Hospital has also performed a pioneering minimally invasive procedure for the treatment of mitral regurgitation. It is hoped that this procedure will help patients with functional mitral regurgitation, a condition where the mitral valve leaks due to dilatation of the mitral valve annulus resulting from left ventricular (LV) impairment.

Such patients do not typically undergo valve surgery as there is little evidence that it is effective in this context, and the risks are higher than usual given the LV impairment.

This new treatment involves passing a device (the MONARC™ device, manufactured by Edwards Lifesciences) via the jugular vein into the coronary sinus, a vein that runs around the mitral valve annulus.

The device consists of two anchors and a bridge that is programmed to gradually shorten. This leads to a slow change in the function of the mitral valve, causing a reduction in regurgitation, and potentially an improvement in patient symptoms and outcome.

The procedure is carried out under local anaesthetic and patients can be discharged early after the procedure, usually the next day.

The procedure is currently only carried out as part of a clinical research trial (the EVOLUTION II trial) and Papworth Hospital is the lead centre within the UK. Dr Michael O'Sullivan, the UK chief investigator for the EVOLUTION II trial and a consultant cardiologist at Papworth, carried out the first procedure at Papworth with his consultant colleague, Peter Schofield.

Michael O'Sullivan commented:

Whilst it must be emphasised that this is a new technique, and will not be suitable for everyone, the early results with this device have been promising. There is the potential that this will dramatically impact upon the treatment of patients with mitral valve disease and cardiac failure.

Peter and I are very pleased to be involved with this innovative therapy.

Surgery of the aorta (the body's largest blood vessel as it exits the heart) is carried out to treat or prevent complications such as aneurysm (ballooning out of the artery) and rupture. Papworth carries out more operations on the thoracic aorta than anywhere in the UK.

Arrhythmia surgery is carried out to correct disturbances of heart rhythm. For example, Papworth offers the surgical MAZE procedure for atrial fibrillation.

TAVI

In 2008 Papworth was one of the first centres in the world to offer transcatheter valve implantation and in 2012 it carried out its 75th TAVI.

The purpose of the procedure is to replace the diseased aortic valve without open-heart surgery via a minimally invasive approach.

The majority of patients (70–80 per cent) referred to Papworth will benefit from surgery. Occasionally the type of disease may not be appropriate for surgery, or the patient may be too unwell to undergo the operation. In this circumstance he or she will be followed carefully and there may be some medical treatments available that can help improve the severity of pulmonary hypertension. At present, Papworth Hospital is working closely with other centres around the world to develop more effective treatments for this condition.

Aortic valve stenosis (narrowing) leads to obstruction of blood flow out of the heart. It is the most common form of acquired valvular heart disease in the UK, occurring in 2–4 per cent of adults over 65 years old. It becomes more common with increasing age, so as the population grows older it will become more of a problem. This disease can cause many symptoms such as exercise restriction, breathlessness, chest pain and collapse, as well as premature death. Frequent hospital admissions are often required and overall this can lead to a poor quality of life.

The only proven remedy for the relief of symptoms as well as improved survival is surgery to replace the valve. This is a very established technique with excellent long-term results. However, the risks of major complications or death are much higher in emergency operations, elderly patients, and in patients with concomitant coronary artery disease, kidney failure, and advanced heart failure.

Papworth Hospital offers a TAVI procedure which allows the aortic valve to be replaced without a major chest operation. New transcatheter technologies (where a valve is implanted through a small tube similar to keyhole surgery) mean a heart–lung bypass machine is not required as the operation can be carried out while the heart is beating.

In view of the ageing population and the increasing numbers of patients who could benefit from a more durable procedure, there has been more recent interest in the development of a percutaneously (through the skin) inserted heart valve, avoiding the need for a major operation. Papworth Hospital has been collaborating very closely with Edwards Lifesciences, who have developed a new type of valve which can be implanted via the leg arteries, or through a small incision underneath the left breast. The procedure involves passing a wire across the centre of the narrow valve. This allows the introduction of the artificial SAPIEN™ aortic valve which is mounted and compressed onto a balloon. As the balloon is inflated it opens up the narrowed valve orifice, consequently leading to relief of blood flow obstruction out of the heart.

A team of over 50 people have been involved with the introduction of this groundbreaking technique led by Dr Cameron Densem, consultant interventional cardi-ologist. It has required a multidisciplinary approach and collaboration between many of the hospital departments. The unique position of Papworth Hospital as a leading cen-tre for cardiothoracic medicine has made it an ideal place to adopt these new treatments.

In May 2013 Papworth received national recognition by becoming a nationally commissioned centre for its TAVI. Papworth's pioneering team can now assess patients from anywhere in England with a view to subsequent operation. Dr Cameron Densem, clinical lead for the TAVI service, said:

This is excellent news for Papworth Hospital and reflects the hard work of the Papworth team over the last five years. The first TAVI was performed at Papworth in 2008. Year-on-year patient numbers are increasing and we have now implanted over 100 devices. The results we achieve from these procedures are good and it offers an excellent alternative for those patients considered high-risk for con-ventional aortic valve surgery.

Measuring outcomes

Results of heart surgery at Papworth are continuously and meticulously scrutinised, and survival rates are among the best that can be achieved in the UK and worldwide.

Samer Nashef, who qualified as a doctor at the University of Bristol in 1980, is a consultant cardiac surgeon at Papworth and a world-leading expert on risk and quality in surgical care. He is the creator of EuroSCORE, which calculates the predicted risk of death from heart operations and is the most successful risk model in medicine; it is used worldwide and is credited with saving tens of thousands of lives. Nashef is the author of more than 200 publications, his research has been widely cited, and he has been invited to lecture in more than 30 countries. He is a clinical tutor at the University of Cambridge, and has appeared in NHS Direct videos, at the Wellcome Trust foundation, and in Channel 4's *The Operation*.

EuroSCORE (European System for Cardiac Operative Risk Evaluation) asks for seventeen items of information about the patient, the state of the heart and the proposed operation, and uses logistic regression to calculate the risk of death. It is free to use online. First published in 1999, the model is believed to have contributed substantially to the worldwide improvement in the results of heart surgery seen at the beginning of the millennium. The original models are now ageing and a new model – EuroSCORE II – was announced at the European Association for Cardio-Thoracic Surgery meeting in Lisbon on 3 October 2011 and published in the *European Journal of Cardiothoracic Surgery* in April 2012. The updated calculator is available online at the official EuroSCORE website.

This is what Nashef wrote about the development of EuroSCORE:

I worked with a Frenchman, François Roques, who had already been working on a Parsonnet model for checking performance in France.

'I think you and I can do better', he said.

'Better than what?'

'Better than Parsonnet, better than the French score, better than everything. We should create our own risk model.'

I liked the sound of that, and the two of us agreed to go ahead.

François and I picked out every risk factor known or suspected to influence outcome. We designed a user-friendly, single-sided A4 form to collect the data, with carefully designed wording and explanations. We asked for data on risk factors, the operation performed, and the outcome: was the patient alive or dead afterwards?

We printed out tens of thousands of these forms, packaged them, and sent them to individual hospitals in eight European countries, and recruited one of the best biostatisticians in France, Philippe Michel, of the University of Bordeaux, to do the analysis. After all the data were gathered, some 20,000 patients from 128 hospitals in eight European countries were studied, and information collected on 97 risk factors in all the patients. The data were laboriously transcribed into a computer database at the

University of Bordeaux. We therefore knew the risk profile of the patients, and we knew which had survived. We then flew to Bordeaux to create the risk model. For days, François, Philippe and I studied and validated data, and designed and discarded models.

Finally, in May 1997, we had a model that worked very well and was simple to use, intuitive, and credible. We named it the European System for Cardiac Operative Risk Evaluation (EuroSCORE).

The paper describing EuroSCORE was accepted for presentation at the plenary session of the next meeting of the European Association for Cardio-Thoracic Surgery in Brussels, and I had the privilege of reading the paper to a packed house. A few weeks later, the full paper was published in the association's journal.

The success of EuroSCORE exceeded our wildest expectations. The model has been used globally, in every continent and in almost every country with cardiac surgery. The paper alone has been cited in more than 2,300 scientific publications, and the term EuroSCORE has entered the medical vocabulary. The risk model that it refers to has been used for decision-making about the risk of surgery, for evaluating the quality of care, for predicting death (which it was designed to do), for comparing the results of surgery, for predicting complications (which it was not designed to do), and for estimating the cost and length of hospitalisation. In some countries, it has even entered the legal system, so that the family of a heart surgery patient with a low EuroSCORE is automatically compensated if he or she dies.

Now that we have a risk model, how do we put it into practice?

When a risk model allows us to predict the likely outcome, we immediately have a benchmark against which we can compare the actual outcome. The easiest and most basic use of this tool is for the monitoring of surgical performance using hospital mortality (death from the operation).

Most patients admitted to hospital for a heart operation, or any other kind of operation, are alive when they enter hospital. Very rarely, a patient arrives dead but 'warm', and is brought back to life by a heart operation, but this is extremely rare. We can therefore safely assume that virtually all patients having a heart operation are alive when they come in to hospital, and most will be alive when they leave hospital after the operation. The difference between the number coming in alive and the number leaving alive is the hospital mortality. This is an objective measure, difficult to falsify, and available in the data of almost any hospital, no matter how rudimentary the hospital information system. Thus the hospital mortality can be expressed as a percentage: if 100 patients enter the hospital alive, and 98 leave the hospital alive, then the actual mortality is 2 per cent.

A risk model such as EuroSCORE allows us to predict what that mortality should be on average, taking into account the risk profile of the patients. By adding up the EuroSCOREs for all 100 patients together, and dividing by 100, we have another percentage, and that is the average predicted mortality.

The next step is to compare the two. If a particular hospital's actual mortality is 1 per cent and its predicted mortality is 2 per cent, can we conclude that this hospital is doing better than predicted? No, we can't. We can be pretty sure that the hospital is doing no worse than predicted, but, to be able to say that it is actually doing better than predicted, we need to be confident that the result isn't likely to be due to chance.

When we look at data, we very rarely look at the entire data from the population that interests us. Most of the time, we collect a sample of data, and hope that the findings in that sample reflect those in the whole population. The reason is simple: it is usually difficult and time-consuming to measure anything in a whole population. Say, for example, you wanted to find out the average height of people in your town. You could line them all up and measure them, but that would take a huge effort and a very long time, especially if your town is London or Melbourne. Much easier would be to take a random sample of a few hundred folk in your town and measure them, and hope that your sample is representative of the whole population. How confident can you be that the measurement you took actually reflects the real average height of all the townsfolk? The statisticians have a very good method to answer that question, and that is what is called the 'confidence interval'. In a way, this is also analogous to decisions made in law. Like a judge asking a jury to be sure beyond reasonable doubt that the accused is guilty, stating the confidence interval gives us the range within which we can be certain beyond reasonable doubt that the true value of what we are interested in lies within that range. We now know that the arbitrary cut-off point for certainty in medicine is established. In medical statistics, to be beyond reasonable doubt is to be at least 95 per cent certain.

There is more than one method of working out the confidence interval, and the choice depends on the type of data one is dealing with. If you are measuring the height of people in a population, the distribution of these heights will be 'normal', or, in other words, it follows the well-known shape of the bell curve, with most measurements clustered around the average, and the rest becoming less and less frequent on either side of the average.

Certain events, such as death after heart surgery, happen rarely, say 2 per cent of the time. If we look at many patient groups, and plot all the mortalities on a graph, we do not get a normal distribution, or a bell curve. Instead, we get a skewed distribution, with most measured mortalities clustered around 0–4 per cent, then a long and diminishing 'tail' of higher mortalities. This sort of distribution is called a Poisson distribution, named after the 19th-century French mathematician Siméon Poisson.

With the introduction of EuroSCORE to predict the mortality of surgery with reasonable accuracy, surgeons at last had a standard against which they could assess their own performance. They were no longer in the dark when it came to knowing how well or badly they were doing. The Hawthorne effect [when behaviour is modified in response to being monitored] swung into action, and the inevitable happened. The results of cardiac surgery improved worldwide, and the greatest improvements were seen in those countries that had the most robust measurement systems. As a cause-and-effect phenomenon, this is impossible to prove. As a general rule, medicine, like everything else, gets better with time, and the improvements that followed the introduction of EuroSCORE could merely have been part and parcel of this natural progress, but the size and timing of these improvements in cardiac surgery were truly remarkable.

EuroSCORE was published in 1999 and had gained widespread acceptance in the ensuing one or two years. By 2002, a mere two to three years later, the mortality of heart surgery in many centres and in many countries had almost halved, despite the fact that older and sicker patients were being operated on. In the UK, heart surgery results are now closely monitored, scrutinised, and constantly compared with EuroSCORE prediction, and the results are published on the worldwide web for all to see (www.scts.org). The UK now boasts cardiac surgery survival rates that are among the best in the world, and if the Hawthorne effect did indeed play a part in this improvement, then EuroSCORE, a mere risk model, could be justifiably claimed to have saved up to 6,000 lives in the UK alone so far. (Nobel Prize nominating committee, please note!) Survival rates in other countries have also shown a massive improvement since the introduction of performance measurement, and the likely number of lives saved worldwide is probably several times larger.

By 2005, reports were trickling in from some institutions that actual mortality was a lot lower than the EuroSCORE model predicted. During the following two to three years, the trickle became a flood. The model was still excellent at distinguishing between a low-risk and a high-risk patient, but its ability to measure the magnitude of that risk was inaccurate across the board. There was nothing to do but create another model, and that is exactly what we did. François Roques and I formed a new team to work on this venture, and were joined by Linda Sharples, then Medical Research Council statistician in Cambridge, now Professor of Statistics in Leeds. We collected data on more than 20,000 patients from hundreds of hospitals in over 50 countries of all continents, and recreated the model with contemporary data. This model (EuroSCORE II) is now available, and early signs indicate that the cardiac surgical community has adopted it enthusiastically.

One of the tasks of the EuroSCORE II project was to find out what exactly is a death. This is not a facetious comment. I alluded earlier to the fact that, after an operation, even death can be difficult to define. The following can all, with varying degrees of legitimacy, lay claim to the title 'early postoperative death'. If the patient dies on the operating table, there is no argument: it is an operative death. If the patient survives the operation, but dies two days later, most people would agree that this is an 'early' or postoperative death. We can also define survival or death as the state that the patient is in when leaving the hospital after an operation, as this is clear and cannot be argued with, but what if the patient never leaves hospital, and goes on to die in hospital six years after an operation? Is that still a postoperative or early death? An alternative would be to say the patient is considered to have survived the operation if he or she is still alive 30 days after the operation, but even that has problems.

First, it is not much use to the patient if an operation results in complications, and the patient stays on the intensive care unit being supported by increasingly desperate measures and expensive high-tech equipment, until death occurs on day 31. Second, some patients go home and die a few days later, but by then they are no longer under the beady eye of the hospital audit department, and whoever is collecting the mortality data may never find out about the tragic events that can happen after hospital discharge. This is further complicated by the fact that many people, like Professor Paul Sergeant of Leuven in Belgium, believe, with good justification from survival data, that the true attrition rate for death after an operation does not truly level out until 90 days after an operation, not 30 days. Ninety days is an awfully long time for an audit department to track the patients, some of whom may have moved house, emigrated, or simply no longer want to stay in touch with their treating hospital because they have better things to do. Hospitals, like all organisations, are not awash with money, and many other priorities compete for their limited resources with greater clamour than the chasing of old patients around the country and beyond to see how they have fared after leaving hospital.

We therefore looked at the data that the hospitals gave us in the EuroSCORE II study, and found that all hospitals could give us 100 per cent of the data on the status of the patient on leaving hospital (dead or alive). When it came to 30 days, just over half the hospitals had data. When it came to 90 days, the proportion dropped to below half. We therefore took a drastic decision, and defined an early death as one that occurs in the same hospital during the same admission as the operation. This was arbitrary and pragmatic: these data we knew were both available and accurate, important features to consider when one chooses a benchmark. We can still learn valuable lessons from those hospitals that actually had data on patients after they left hospital. These data were very valuable in that they helped us to find out what was the attrition rate after discharge from hospital: we found that, if the mortality is 4 per cent, at 30 days it rises by another 0.6 per cent and, at 90 days, by another 0.9 per cent. As we know that the rate levels off afterwards, we can postulate that these additional risks should be proportionately taken into account when you decide to have an operation. A little risk still lingers up to 90 days, and thereafter you are probably safe. This is something to bear in mind if you ever find yourself contemplating an operation and weighing up the risks versus the benefit: most of the risk will be concentrated in the time you are an in-patient in hospital, but there is still a little bit left to go through after you go home, and this levels out when you reach 90 days.

Heart surgery today mostly has its house in order. There are at last robust and objective monitoring tools to measure the quality of surgery, even if they simply focus on the relatively crude outcome of survival. These tools are sufficient to detect underperformance, and can provide the information and impetus necessary to correct such underperformance. In the current era, a poor hospital or a rogue surgeon with terrible results will be either corrected or stopped from operating. In the United Kingdom and in many other countries, data on outcomes are routinely measured, and action is taken as soon as the data indicate substandard performance. If you seek the treatment of heart surgery for yourself or a loved one in the United Kingdom, you may not receive the best in the country, but you will certainly receive treatment that is up to a high international standard regardless of which hospital or surgeon you choose, and that is surely a comforting thought. Similar monitoring in other countries also goes a long way to ensure that heart surgery there is also likely to be of a safe standard. In general, the more robust is the monitoring system, the safer is the surgery. Other surgical and medical specialties do not at present have anything like the level of monitoring that heart surgery has, but they are most certainly working, with varying degrees of reluctance, towards developing similar systems. My prediction is that it will not be long before all medical specialties will have robust monitoring and outcome measurements, and, when that happens, the Hawthorne effect will come into action, and the results and success of intervention in these specialties are likely to show a similar quantum leap in performance to that seen in heart surgery.

Sir Terence English, KBE, FRCS, FRCP, past President of the Royal College of Surgeons of England and, as we have

seen, the surgeon who carried out the first heart transplant
in the UK, wrote as the Foreword to Nashef's book:

I had the pleasure of being a colleague of Samer Nashef
after his appointment as a consultant at Papworth
Hospital in 1992. It soon became apparent that we had
added an unusually gifted and stimulating surgeon to our
team. He already had a wide experience across the field
of adult cardiac surgery, and was a fine technical surgeon
and wise clinician. He also had the habit of questioning
received wisdom, which encouraged us to look critically
at procedures and see how these could be improved.

In due course, the latter propensity became a driving
ambition to help cardiac surgeons to become more trans-
parent about their results. This in turn led to creating the
EuroSCORE model for predicting the outcome of heart
operations, so that individual and national groups of surgeons could compare their results. The model became
widely applied across Europe and beyond, and acted as
an important stimulus for improving the results of cardiac
surgery, thereby saving many lives.

Nashef's book gives interesting examples of his investigations into factors affecting outcomes, such as whether
surgeons should operate immediately after a death on
the table, and whether the risk-propensity of individual
surgeons is measurable and can affect their results. He
has a gift for making complex issues understandable, and
presents the means by which patients can use mortality
data to help them come to informed decisions about the
risks and benefits of treatments offered them. At a more

general level, he provides powerful arguments against some of the ill-conceived targets and rankings created by non-professionals that hospitals have been subjected to, and shows how these can mislead patients and demoralise doctors.

The Naked Surgeon is altogether a very stimulating read and one that will be of great interest to both patients and doctors. It should also receive the attention it deserves from health politicians, hospital managers, and health economists.

Surgeons at Papworth routinely review the survival of their patients after heart surgery. Every month, the results of the previous twelve months are examined. Survival is compared with the national results and assessed with regard to casemix (how old and sick the patients are).

Survival for all operations, including casemix, repeat, multiple and emergency operations, was 97.7 per cent and survival for non-emergency operations was 98.3 per cent.

In the year to November 2014, survival for all operations (including complex, repeat, multiple, urgent and emergency and salvage operations) was 98.1 per cent and survival for elective operations was 98.9 per cent.

Samer Nashef noted that:

Heart surgery in the UK is now so good that, as a whole, British hospitals have death rates which are constantly lower than standard risk models predict, but even taking this into account cardiac surgery mortality at Papworth this year was less than half the expected mortality in comparison with the most recent British results.

Stephen Bridge, Chief Executive at Papworth, added:

> Patients choose to come to Papworth because, as an inter-national centre of excellence, we are able to attract the best, most highly skilled staff and deliver the very best results for our patients.

Chest medicine

Of course, Papworth Hospital has, since its foundation 100 years ago and its concentration on TB, always been deeply involved in chest medicine.

The hospital's chest physicians manage acute and chronic respiratory conditions in collaboration with specialist radiologists and histopathologists. The Chest Department has a number of sub-specialist services, many of which have a regional or national caseload. These include services for patients with: cystic fibrosis; recurrent lung infections including those with bronchiectasis and immunodeficiency (Cambridge Centre for Lung Infection (CCLI)); interstitial lung disease and pulmonary vascular diseases; the thoracic oncology (lung cancer) service; the ataxia telangiectasia service; services for patients with pulmonary fibrosis, vasculitis, and rare diseases including Wegener's granulomatosis and pulmonary alveolar proteinosis.

Mesothelioma

In June 2012 it was announced: 'Papworth opens meso-thelioma cancer research centre, believed to be the first in Europe.'

What is mesothelioma?

Mesothelioma is a malignant tumour involving the pleura (lining of the lung). The symptoms are a dry cough, shortness of breath, chest pain, fatigue, weight loss or, more rarely, difficulty with swallowing, hoarseness and nerve pain. It is a rare and terminal cancer caused mainly by asbestos and can take decades to develop.

To make a diagnosis, doctors will usually withdraw fluid from the chest cavity or perform a thorascopy, to drain the fluid from the chest cavity to extract a biopsy.

The centre will bring together information for researchers and doctors tackling mesothelioma. The 'Mesobank' will hold live tissue samples and anonymous clinical data. Project leader Dr Robert Rintoul, consultant physician at Papworth, said it would greatly improve research into a 'neglected cancer'.

The annual number of mesothelioma deaths in the UK has nearly quadrupled in the last 30 years and the UK now has the highest mortality rates of any country in the world. It kills around 2,300 UK residents each year – more than cervical cancer, testicular cancer, thyroid cancer, mouth cancer and malignant melanoma – according to the Health and Safety Executive.

Rintoul said: 'In research terms, mesothelioma has been a neglected cancer for far too long. The opening of the Mesobank could really help change this, by making it quicker, easier and cheaper for researchers to undertake the kind of research that could deliver real advances in our understanding and treatment of this devastating disease.'

The facility was set up by the British Lung Foundation and the Mick Knighton Mesothelioma Research Fund.

Cystic fibrosis

In the early days of cystic fibrosis most young patients did not survive into adult life and thus services were provided in paediatric hospitals. The few adult patients were treated in general chest clinics but, as care improved with the availability of better antibiotics and an emphasis on nutrition, the number of cystic fibrosis patients increased. Some came to lung transplantation. It became apparent that specialist care would further the longevity and well-being of these patients and so a specialist in- and out-patient service was developed at Papworth in the 1980s by Di Bilton.

Papworth, in collaboration with Medical School colleges, continues to advance care for cystic fibrosis patients and to influence future care for patients, many of whom now reach middle age.

Lung cancer

There is universal agreement, following the Calman recommendations that systems are in place that allow an effective and efficient pathway of care for patients with suspected cancer of the lung, that all forms of cancer are best managed in multidisciplinary teams, providing specialist input from thoracic surgeons, radiotherapists, oncologists, specialist nurses, therapists and palliative care specialists. Surgery should of course be carried out at specialist cardiothoracic facilities, but the issue of diagnosis, oncological treatment and palliative management must involve those who work in primary care and professionals within local acute hospitals.

RSSC

Papworth Hospital also has the largest Respiratory Support and Sleep Centre (RSSC) in the UK.

An important consultant at Papworth was the recently retired Dr John Shneerson. His specialist clinical interests were respiratory failure due to COPD (chronic obstructive pulmonary disease), neuromuscular and skeletal disorders including spinal cord injury, sleep apnoea, narcolepsy, restless legs syndrome, sleepwalking and other physical activities during sleep. His research interests were treatment of respiratory failure, particularly with non-invasive ventilation, physiology and treatment of sleep disorders.

The RSSC provides services for patients with sleep disorders (including common disorders such as obstructive sleep apnoea and less common ones such as narcolepsy) and those with ventilatory failure (from conditions such as COPD or neuromuscular disorders including motor neuron disease and poliomyelitis). The service provides non-invasive ventilation and also accepts referrals from other intensive care units to wean patients from invasive ventilation.

TCCA

TCCA (Theatres, Critical Care and Anaesthesia Services) supports all surgical activity across the hospital and comprises the following departments: Theatres, Critical Care, Anaesthesia, Sterile Services and Technical Support Services.

In intensive care medicine, extracorporeal membrane

oxygenation (commonly abbreviated to ECMO) or extracorporeal life support (ECLS) is an extracorporeal ('outside
the body') technique of providing both cardiac and respiratory support to patients whose heart and lungs are
so severely diseased or damaged that they can no longer
serve their function. Initial cannulation of a patient receiving ECMO is performed by a surgeon or anaesthetist and
maintenance of the patient is the responsibility of the per-
fusionist or ECMO specialist who gives 24/7 monitoring
care for the duration of the ECMO treatment.

ECMO is a technique that oxygenates blood by pumping
it through a machine outside of the body. It can be used
in potentially reversible severe respiratory failure when
conventional ventilation is unable to oxygenate the blood
adequately. The aim of ECMO in respiratory failure is to
allow the injured lung to recover while avoiding certain
recognised complications associated with conventional
ventilation.

ECMO can also, in some circumstances, support the
heart by circulating the blood around the body when the
heart is too weak to do this.

TCCA covers the hospital's provision of ECMO services.
Papworth is one of only five UK hospitals to provide this
service.

Critical Care (CCA) at Papworth believes in putting
patients at the centre of critical care services. High value is
placed on evidence-based nursing care, good communica-
tion, a supportive professional atmosphere, and the belief
that these underpin the delivery of high-quality care in an
advanced technological environment. Attention to detail

and pride in the unit by all staff is essential to ensure that an exemplary standard is maintained.

The Critical Care Unit comprises five bays and includes six single rooms, giving a total of 29 beds. Patients go to intensive care in high-dependency beds according to their clinical need. Intensive care patients are nursed 1:1, and the nursing ratio for high-dependency patients varies between 1:2 and 1:3 depending on the patients. Most of the patients who come to Critical Care have had planned major heart surgery. The most common operations performed are coronary artery bypass surgery (CABG) and valve replacements. The majority of these patients are cared for within the Cardiac Recovery Unit (which is within one of the bays of Critical Care). This is a specially designated area for overnight care of patients following surgery. The aim is that they are transferred back to the ward the following day or, if requiring further intervention, are transferred to the Critical Care Area. In addition to this routine work, the unit also admits patients following other major surgery including heart and lung transplants and thoracic aortic aneurysm repair, patients requiring cardiac assist devices and patients following pulmonary endarterectomy surgery (PEA). The unit will also take any patient from within the hospital with organ failure.

All staff working within Critical Care undergo a comprehensive training programme to help equip them for nursing in this specialised field. Critical and managerial practice is guided by procedures and guidelines to help ensure that a common good standard of practice is maintained throughout the unit.

Thoracic surgery

Thoracic surgery has evolved over the past 40 to 50 years since the days of TB surgery. As cardiac surgery expanded, in many centres and at Papworth, thoracic surgery was combined with a cardiac surgery practice. For many years, following the retirement of Ben Milstein, this has been led at Papworth by Francis Wells.

There were thoracic surgeons in Norwich and gradually many other centres appointed pure thoracic surgeons as the work expanded and diversified. Papworth now has three full-time thoracic surgeons intimately involved with chest treatment and offers a comprehensive lung cancer service and other diagnostic and curative surgical operations.

As technology has developed, and particularly in the last ten years, many of the operations are now performed through incision in the chest with sophisticated imaging technology and instruments.

Papworth specialises in the following:

- Lung cancer
- Complex lung resections
- Minimal access surgery
- Surgery for patients with reduced lung function
- Investigation and management of pleural diseases
- Chest wall surgery
- Pectus surgery
- Airway surgery
- Surgery for the mediastinum
- Metastasectomy
- Thoracic sarcoma

Provision was traditionally split almost 50/50 between Norwich and Papworth. All intrathoracic conditions were dealt with at Papworth, including pulmonary, mediastinal and oesophageal surgery, along with minor procedures such as oesophagoscopies and thoracoscopies. Oesophageal surgery is no longer performed at Papworth as it is now the domain of gastrointestinal surgeons at Addenbrooke's. The successful development of the lung cancer centre has recently led to an increase in complex major/major procedures. Thoracic surgeons are involved in the management of patients with major trauma in the larger local acute hospitals with Accident & Emergency centres. Management of acute trauma is important but does not constitute a significant proportion of the specialty's total workload. Thoracic surgeons from Papworth hold out-patient clinics at Addenbrooke's, Bedford, Hinchingbrooke, Ipswich, Peterborough and West Suffolk Hospitals.

There are three consultant surgeons and they work closely with ten other cardiothoracic surgeons in providing a 24-hour thoracic surgery service.

CT scanner

When the CT scanner was installed at Papworth in December 2014, the *Cambridge News* wrote:

> The SOMATOM Force, a £1.5 million Siemens CT scanner, has been installed at the UK's leading cardiothoracic hospital – and is the first of its kind in the UK.
>
> An official launch was held yesterday to commemorate this significant step forward in diagnostic care at Papworth

Hospital with a demonstration of the CT scanner. Julian Huppert said: 'I am delighted to have been given the opportunity to unveil the latest CT scanning technology at Papworth Hospital today. It is essential that the clinical teams have the most cutting-edge equipment available to them to give patients the best diagnosis and treatment. This paired with the Trust's international reputation in cardiothoracic care is the reason that the hospital's move to Cambridge is so important and a campaign that I continue to support.'

The scanner would not only improve diagnostic care at Papworth Hospital with state-of-the-art 4D scanning technology but also dramatically reduce the level of radiation patients were exposed to – just a fifth of the average CT scanner.

This would open up the use of the CT scanner to more patients including those with shortness of breath, who would otherwise have been deemed unsuitable for such a scan.

Bobby Agrawal, Consultant Radiologist at Papworth Hospital, said: 'This exciting cutting edge scanning technology will enhance diagnosis in a wide range of patients with significantly decreased radiation dose and with much shorter scanning times, further increasing the utility of CT in patients who were previously unsuitable for CT including young patients with chronic diseases who require frequent CT imaging.'

With a top rotation speed of four turns per second (0.25 seconds per rotation) the Force will also reduce the length of time a scan takes and therefore increase the number of patients who can be seen during clinics at Papworth.

Chapter 8

PULMONARY HYPERTENSION

Prostacyclin
Nitric oxide
Pulmonary thromboendarterectomy and endarterectomy
Heart failure service

Prostacyclin

Pulmonary hypertension is an increase of blood pressure in the pulmonary artery, pulmonary vein, or pulmonary capillaries, together known as the lung vasculature, leading to shortness of breath, dizziness, fainting, leg swelling and other symptoms. Pulmonary hypertension can be a severe disease with a markedly decreased exercise tolerance and outcomes such as heart failure. It was first identified by Ernst von Romberg in 1891.

Dr Keith McNeil, who took over the research into and treatment of pulmonary hypertension from Tim Higenbottam, noted that Papworth achieved a number of firsts in new treatments, notably prostacyclin, thanks largely to Tim Higenbottam.

McNeil is an internationally recognised expert in the fields of lung transplantation and pulmonary vascular disease. He spent two years as a senior consultant at Papworth and another five years working at both Papworth and Cambridge University Hospitals as a cardiopulmonary transplant and respiratory physician and director of the pulmonary vascular disease unit. He was pivotal in establishing the UK's centre for pulmonary endarterectomy at Papworth and was also an adviser to the Department of Health on pulmonary hypertension.

During the 1960s, a UK research team, headed by Professor Sir John Vane, began to explore the role of prostaglandins in anaphylaxis and respiratory diseases. Working with a team from the Royal College of Surgeons, Sir John discovered that aspirin and other oral anti-inflammatory drugs work by inhibiting the synthesis of prostaglandins.

This critical finding opened the door to a broader understanding of the role of prostaglandins in the body.

Sir John and a team from the Wellcome Foundation had identified a lipid mediator they called 'PG-X', which inhibits platelet aggregation. PG-X, which later would become known as prostacyclin, is 30 times more potent than any other then-known anti-aggregatory agent.

Right heart cardiac catheterisation is performed in the main for patients with primary pulmonary hypertension who may go on to long-term prostacyclin infusion therapy. It has been found that self-administered continuous 24-hour infusion of prostacyclin has considerably improved the quality of life of many of these patients, has avoided pre-terminal syncope and has 'bought time' for some patients who would otherwise die before receiving a transplant. For this therapy patients who had failed to improve on conventional vasodilator therapy, and whose mixed venous oxygenation had been less than 63 per cent, were selected. These patients had a 17 per cent three-year survival chance untreated. It has been possible to improve their exercise tolerance and prevent dangerous syncopal episodes. Many of these patients improved sufficiently to allow their transfer from the provisional waiting list. The progress of primary pulmonary hypertension was not reversed, however, and ultimately they either died or required heart–lung transplantation. Nevertheless, this therapy improved the one-year survival from 37 per cent to 68 per cent. Long-term prostacyclin therapy is an expensive form of treatment and is reserved for those who have failed to improve on conventional vasodilator drugs. It provides only a temporary respite in the progressive deterioration towards death.

Nitric oxide

Papworth pioneered the use of inhaled nitric oxide for selected patients with pulmonary hypertension.

Nitric oxide, or nitrogen oxide, also known as nitrogen monoxide, is a molecule with chemical formula NO. It is a free radical and is an important intermediate in the chemical industry. Nitric oxide is a by-product of combustion of substances in the air, as in automobile engines and fossil fuel power plants, and is produced naturally during the electrical discharges of lightning in thunderstorms.

Nitric oxide should not be confused with nitrous oxide (N_2O), an anaesthetic and greenhouse gas, or with nitrogen dioxide (NO_2), a brown toxic gas and a major air pollutant. However, nitric oxide is rapidly oxidised in air to nitrogen dioxide. Humphry Davy discovered this to his discomfort, when he inhaled the gas early in his career.

Despite being a simple molecule, NO is an important biological regulator and is therefore a fundamental component in the fields of neuroscience, physiology, and immunology. It was proclaimed 'Molecule of the Year' in 1992. Research into its function led to the 1998 Nobel Prize for discovering the role of nitric oxide as a cardiovascular signalling molecule.

Pulmonary thromboendarterectomy and endarterectomy

Papworth is one of the four UK pulmonary hypertension centres and the only one providing pulmonary thromboendarterectomy. A programme for this operation was started in 1996 when it was practised on people awaiting heart transplants to keep them alive long enough for a suitable donor heart to become available. Six were carried out, with three survivals, led by John Dunning with great support from John Wallwork. The six operations in the first year were gradually built up to twelve then to 25 and then on to 60 a year, with a constantly improving survival rate. David Jenkins currently leads the team involved.

David Jenkins trained in cardiac surgery on the West London rotation and was appointed as consultant at Papworth Hospital in 2001.

A pulmonary thromboendarterectomy (PTE) has significant risk; mortality for the operation is typically 5 per cent, but less in centres with high volume and experience. PTEs are risky because of what is done and how it is done. PTEs involve a full cardiopulmonary bypass, deep hypothermia and full cardiac arrest, with the critical procedure carried out in a standstill operation.

The reason for the complexity of procedure comes from the anatomy. The obvious part is that a pulmonary bypass is required. Surgeons cannot operate on something they cannot see; the blood going to the lungs has to be diverted from the pulmonary vasculature and lung function taken care of by a machine. Less obvious is that hypothermia is required. This relates to the pathophysiology of emboli; they are organised, somewhat delicate, essentially part of the vessel wall, and hard to remove completely, unlike in an acute pulmonary embolectomy (for acute pulmonary embolism, which is done without hypothermia). Making this task more difficult is the anatomy of the lung and pathophysiology of chronic thromboembolic pulmonary hypertension (CTEPH); lungs also get blood from the bronchial arteries which are often enlarged. The practical implication is that a conventional cardiopulmonary bypass operation is not sufficient to do the surgery because too much blood would be in the surgical field and the delicate thrombi would be difficult to remove completely.

The solution is a full cardiac arrest, which can be done with hypothermia. So, after going on to CPB they induce a deep hypothermia, cooling the patient to 18–20°C, to preserve the patient's brain. Once the patient is cooled off sufficiently the CPB machine is turned off and the surgeon has time to do the delicate work, which takes about 40 minutes, and consists of carefully removing the organised thrombus. The most challenging part of the surgery is finding the optimal plane to dissect the pulmonary artery. If the surgeon dissects too deeply into the vessel wall the pulmonary vessels may rupture. If the surgeon does not dissect deep enough the clot breaks proximally during extraction and the distal part of the pulmonary vasculature will not have its pulmonary blood flow restored. The right lung is typically done first. At the end an almost beautiful negative of the pulmonary arteries exists – as the emboli over time fill the larger vessels that feed the smaller occluded vessel. It is not uncommon that collectively this negative almost represents the whole pulmonary tree – the only part missing being what the person was living off before the surgery. Bypass time is typically five and a half hours.

The benefits of PTEs are significant. Most patients after surgery no longer suffer from shortness of breath and therefore have a much improved quality of life. Because the obstruction in the lung vessels has been removed, the resistance to blood flow drops to normal levels. Further, pulmonary vascular resistance (PVR) usually drops back to close to normal levels. This in turn means that the work of the heart decreases and, as a result, patients are spared from further damage to the right ventricle, which in this case is the cardiac output. As a result of the operation, patients are spared from pulmonary hypertension and further right ventricular hypertrophy. Most pleasing is that patients who previously had right heart dysfunction often recover function.

The University of California San Diego Medical Centre's cardiothoracic surgery department, led by Dr Stuart Jamieson, is widely recognised as a pioneer in this relatively new surgery, having performed more PTEs than the rest of the world combined (over 3,000 since 1970 out of a total of 4,500 worldwide), with the lowest mortality rate (now approximately 1 per cent).

CTEPH is a form of pulmonary hypertension that occurs as the result of blood clots blocking off the arteries of the lungs. While most of these blood clots originate in the veins, many people with this condition may be unaware that these clots are forming. Over time, the blood clots build up in the blood vessels of the lungs, which become permanently scarred with narrowing and decreased blood flow. This results over time in increased pressure and resistance to blood flow in the lungs, leading to pulmonary hypertension and right heart failure. When severe, this situation leads to increasing breathlessness, exercise limitation and reduced life expectancy.

CTEPH was first described in the UK in 1951. It is now more widely recognised and develops in up to 3.8 per cent of patients after acute pulmonary embolism. CTEPH leads to functional impairment and confers a poor prognosis, but many patients can be cured by pulmonary endarterectomy (PEA), having substantial improvement in symptoms and survival.

What is a pulmonary endarterectomy?

PEA is a surgical operation in which the blood vessels of the lungs are cleared of clot and scar material, and it usually takes no less than eight to ten hours. The patient is attached to a heart–lung bypass machine prior to their body temperature being cooled to 20°C, which reduces the body's oxygen requirement and provides protection to organs of the body during the surgery. During the critical part of the surgery where the clots are removed, the heart–lung bypass machine is turned off for up to 20 minutes to create a bloodless field. At this point there is no blood circulation, no heartbeat and no brain activity. The bypass machine is then turned back on to re-perfuse the body's organs again before it is turned off to remove the clots and scarring from the other lung. Research led by the Papworth PEA Team has shown that this is the safest way to perform the operation.

Although the operation sounds simple, it is actually technically very difficult to get access to the arteries of the lungs, and the procedure itself is a major undertaking. For this reason it is necessary to ensure that patients who might potentially benefit from this operation are thoroughly evaluated. Not everyone with CTEPH will be suitable for this operation, and a number of additional investigations must be performed in order to assess the appropriateness of surgery and the level of risk involved. Previously, the lung needed to be removed and a transplant carried out.

The hospital says that 95 per cent of patients with chronic pulmonary hypertension (high blood pressure) survive the operation, carried out at Papworth since 2000.

At a meeting at Jesus College, Cambridge, experts in pulmonary hypertension from across the UK took part to learn about the procedure and celebrate the surgical milestone of the PEA operation. The procedure was initially carried out at only two other centres in Europe – one in Italy and one in France. It takes one day to perform the operation and two procedures each week are carried out at Papworth.

Mr David Jenkins, consultant cardiothoracic surgeon at Papworth, said at the time: 'It is very rewarding to see patients who were extremely ill and previously struggled for breath, able to walk and enjoy their lives after the surgery. It is one of the biggest operations we perform, but results in a dramatic improvement in both quality of life and survival.'

Dr Joanna Pepke-Zaba from the pulmonary hypertension (PH) service said: 'Fifteen years ago, PH was a diagnosis with no real treatment. The situation is far more positive now and treatments have improved beyond measure.

'This operation, because of its complex nature, is carried out in only a few centres, Papworth being the only centre in the UK at the moment. The number of operations, as they became more successful, has risen and the total is now over 100 a year.'

Heart failure service

In the UK, the sub-specialty of heart failure was slow to develop; where it did exist it was mainly the domain of academic clinicians. Through the 1990s and the early years of the new millennium, new treatments that significantly improved prognosis were introduced, including beta blockade and cardiac resynchronisation therapy (CRT).

By the mid-1990s the transplant programme at Papworth had been in existence for about fifteen years. It was recognised that many patients referred for transplantation had not been optimally treated for heart failure and a transplant evaluation could not really be carried out in these circumstances. It was also recognised that many patients who could potentially benefit from a heart transplant were never referred to a transplant centre. It was felt that one way of capturing this population was to develop a heart failure service from which patients could be triaged into the transplant programme at the appropriate time. The service proved popular, not least with the patients who often had not received continuity in their follow-up. The service has been constrained by the time available to the single cardiologist running it, and latterly by lack of out-patient space as well.

Heart transplantation changed in the UK with a change in the way donor organs were allocated and the introduction of an 'Urgent List' in 1999. This essentially consisted of the patients who were most at need and usually those who were confined to intensive care units while supported with inotropic medication (drugs that affect the contraction of the heart muscle) and the intra-aortic balloon pump.

231

Around the same time Papworth introduced a mechanical support programme with short-term and more durable devices which could support patients at home. The sole cardiologist attached to the transplant programme was charged with admitting these patients who were critically ill and assessing their suitability for mechanical support (as a bridge to heart transplantation). The long-term follow-up of these patients was also a time-consuming task.

Over the last ten years the proportion of heart transplants in the UK carried out in critically ill patients has increased to 70 per cent of the total. Papworth, like other transplant centres, is now inundated with requests for the transfer of patients to its intensive care unit for management of advanced heart failure. Most cardiologists with an interest in heart failure do not get involved in the care of such patients once they need intensive care. Most intensive care physicians have experience of dealing with some aspects of the care of such patients but are not used to thinking strategically about the management of these very ill people. The specialty of Intensive Care Cardiology is developing to fill this need; at Papworth, the cardiologists with an interest in advanced heart failure now spend a significant portion of their time in intensive care working with cardiac surgeons and the intensive care team.

Over the last ten years Papworth has introduced continuous flow mechanical pumps (Left Ventricular Assist Devices or LVADs) that can support patients at home for years. The heart failure cardiologist has had to evolve into a VAD physician. Most patients with LVADs continue to need heart failure therapy; this is directed at the unsupported right ventricle and used to promote reverse remodelling of the supported left ventricle.

A VAD is an electromechanical circulatory device that is used to replace partially or completely the function of a failing heart. The function of VADs differs from that of artificial cardiac pacemakers. Some VADs are intended for short-term use, typically for patients recovering from heart attacks or heart surgery, while others are intended for long-term use (months to years and in some cases for life), typically for patients suffering from advanced congestive heart failure.

VADs are distinct from artificial hearts, which are designed to completely take over cardiac function and generally require the removal of the patient's heart. VADs are designed to assist either the right (RVAD) or left (LVAD) ventricle, or both at once (BiVAD). The type that is used depends primarily on the underlying heart disease and the pulmonary arterial resistance that determines the load on the right ventricle.

LVADs are most commonly used, but when pulmonary arterial resistance is high, right ventricular assistance may become necessary. Long-term VADs are normally used to keep patients alive with a good quality of life while they wait for a heart transplantation (known as a 'bridge to transplantation'). However, LVADs are sometimes used as long-term therapy, meaning the patient will never undergo heart transplant, and sometimes as a bridge to recovery.

In the last few years, VADs have improved significantly in terms of providing survival and quality of life among recipients.

The history of heart failure cardiology at Papworth has been unusual in that the specialty developed from the heart transplant programme and has evolved as the advances in surgical treatment of heart failure have thrown up new challenges. It remains a challenging but rewarding field of work.

Chapter 9

PUTTING PATIENTS FIRST

'The staff were brilliant!'
Putting patients at the heart
Papworth Village

'The staff were brilliant!'

By 2005, Papworth had achieved a worldwide reputation, not only for heart and lung transplants but for many other services and treatments. It was able to say of itself:

> Papworth Hospital sits at the centre of a regional and national network of hospitals contributing to the care of patients with coronary heart disease and lung disease. Papworth is an internationally recognised heart and lung centre and one of the leading cardiothoracic hospitals in the United Kingdom. It provides a full range of specialist adult services in cardiology, cardiac surgery, thoracic surgery and respiratory medicine and is the country's main heart and lung transplantation centre.
>
> Its primary focus is to provide services to the three million people in Norfolk, Suffolk, Cambridgeshire, Mid and North Bedfordshire and surrounding areas, but Papworth Hospital also receives referrals for certain sub-specialties from all over the UK. Papworth Hospital currently treats around 19,000 in-patients and day cases and sees over 24,000 out-patients each year. It has over 1,300 staff, 224 beds and an annual budget approaching £80 million.
>
> Papworth patients are drawn mainly from a network of nine referring hospitals in Cambridgeshire, Bedfordshire, Suffolk and Norfolk.

Primary Care Trusts outside the network area also referred patients to Papworth Hospital, and patients came from all over the UK for some of the more specialised services. Services were characterised by:

- A focus on coronary heart disease, lung disease and cancer, all of which affect significant numbers of people.
- Rapidly growing levels of demand and activity.
- Demographic change and increase in the numbers of older people needing specialist treatment.
- Use of advanced technologies leading to a new approach to diagnosis and treatment.
- Growing numbers of patients who had diseases that attacked a number of organs and systems that require treatment by a number of specialists simultaneously.
- Rapidly increasing opportunities for learning and development and the sharing of expertise regionally, nationally and internationally.
- A high-profile and expanding clinical research programme heavily dependent on collaborative working with Addenbrooke's, the University of Cambridge (including the School of Clinical Medicine), the Medical Research Council in Cambridge, the Health Economics Research Group at Brunel University, and various commercial organisations.
- An excellent reputation for clinical services and world-class clinicians.

Some 32 different buildings were spread out over the fourteen-acre site, which incorporated all the clinical buildings as well as a central administration unit and offices. There were two nurses' homes, providing 95 accommodation units, and further residential properties away from the main site in the village. A number of houses within Papworth Everard plus several rented houses in neighbouring towns and villages provide additional staff accommodation.

There have been thousands of grateful patients at Papworth Hospital and a number have written letters and articles expressing their gratitude. Here is one from William Gordon:

I was working as an engineering fitter in an electric meter factory about 1967 when a mobile X-ray unit came to check all the staff for tuberculosis. They found that I had a mis-shaped and enlarged heart with an irregular beat. Ipswich hospital took me on board with annual checkups by Dr Barry. When Dr Barry retired in 1979 Dr Petch came from Papworth Hospital to take the clinic in Ipswich and invited me to have tests done at Papworth. I was very keen to have them. The tests revealed I did not have a proper aortic valve. Instead of the three opening flaps that let blood pump through but not back when the pump stroke ended, I had a disc of tissue with a hole in it that let blood pump through but also some flowed back to the heart.

I was checked for suitability of available replacement valves such as pigskin, plastic or metal. Each type had a time scale – for example a pigskin valve guarantee was 10 years and a metal valve up to 40 years. Thankfully a metal valve was deemed suitable and I had a Bjork-Shiley metal valve implant. This procedure was done by Mr B B Milstein and his team on the 7th June 1982 at Papworth Hospital.

When my wife told Mr Milstein he had magic in his hands, he replied something like 'I am only a plumber.' She replied 'You are a real Gentleman Sir.'

I entered Papworth Hospital on Thursday 3rd June 1982 for a Bjork-Shiley aortic valve implant on Monday 7th June and had a weekend to learn what would be needed of me.

In the Surgical Unit Top Floor Ward upstairs in the big house I was encouraged to help my fellow patients recovering from their operations – and learning the procedures certainly helped to make my operation and recovery easier.

The weather was warm and sunny, allowing the fire door to remain open. At times I sat there in the sun reading one of the ward's books, *First Overland* by Tim Slessor, printed in 1975, about the Oxford and Cambridge Overland Expedition to Singapore involving 6 men and two Land Rovers.

When looking out of the ward window at the old building opposite I read a plaque inscribed thus.

'Sir German Siros Woodhead KBE 1855–1921 Professor of Pathology in the University of Cambridge and one of the founders of Papworth Colony. A very gallant gentleman.'

At 9pm I was examined by Dr Hodder who let me listen through his stethoscope to my heart wheezing, and told me my operation would be on Monday morning – a metal valve that clicks but is best and lasts longer. How true and kind Sir! Tomorrow he will show me the Intensive Care Unit (ICU) and will answer any questions I care to ask – X-ray and ECG tomorrow perhaps.

My personal possessions such as my watch, keys, driving licence and money were handed in and I received a receipt for them signed by E H Steele. That sounded like 'Steal' and raised a smile.

Next day, Friday morning, I had an X-ray and Mr Milstein came to see me.

After some rain it was sunny again. I walked to the pond, and watched the fish and the birds flying around there. I spoke with Mr David Haggar, a heart transplant patient; and Mr Peter Hart, also a transplant man, then a Norfolk man with a lung problem. [Peter Hart died in November 2011, 29 years after his transplant, and thus far is Papworth's longest transplant survivor.]

Still Friday, indoors, at tea time the TV was switched on for the first time but by then it was stormy and the lightning interrupted it. The lightning also cut out the electricity but the emergency power immediately took over. We switched the lights off.

The lightning interfered with the monitors, especially Mr Varney's, and caused the staff to run around re-setting them.

The staff were brilliant, not just dealing with the effect of the lightning but in all their work. They were Sister Barker, Staff nurse Othello, Nurse Vanessa (Auntie Nessie), Auxiliary nurse Reed, the male nurse on night shift, the physiotherapist, Norman the domestics chap, and some others whose names I cannot remember. All were kind and helpful.

I took some liquorice allsorts to help me clear my stomach before the operation but then I had laxatives next morning. I hoped the drainage system worked well.

Sunday morning was sunny again so I did some washing and hung it out on the fire escape. My wife and daughter visited almost daily, coming from Felixstowe. My daughter drove the car and they took my washing including bed sheets and pillow cases to wash at home, but I like doing things for myself.

The lads in the ward were starting to get onto their feet so I became more useful. If patients lying in bed tried to raise themselves up by pushing on their elbows this would pull out the chest stitches, requiring treatment sometimes back in the theatre.

Someone had an idea to have a rope for patients to pull themselves upright with, as this tends to close the wound instead of opening it. As there was only one rope I had the job of taking it to whoever needed it in the male ward and to nurses in the female ward. I asked my wife to bring some ropes that I had at home and she did. I scrubbed and disinfected them in the sluice room and there they remained until after my operation.

On the Sunday the anaesthetist came to explain to me all that would happen at the operation, to help me co-operate during the procedures. My wife had asked our friend Mr John Porter, foreman rigger at Felixstowe Docks for more rope. The Docks Manager kindly let us have a whole reel of suitable rope and my wife brought it to Papworth Hospital that day. She usually brought flowers too to brighten the ward.

Monday 7th June 1982 was the operation day. I had noticed earlier that there was a Surgeon and Doctors list in reception that read as follows.

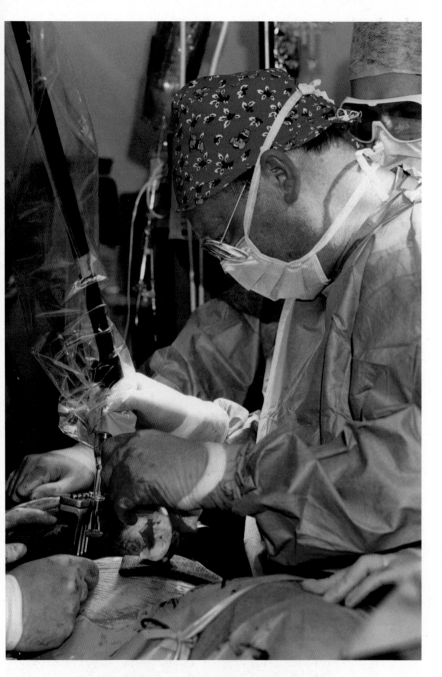

John Wallwork carrying out a heart operation.

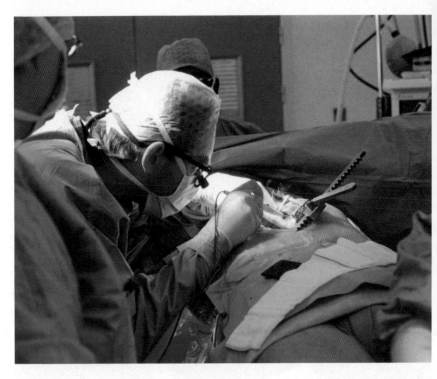

A lung operation.

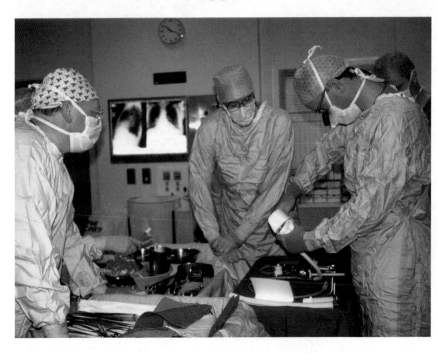

An LVAD operation in progress at Papworth.

David Jenkins is the lead surgeon for the national pulmonary hypertension and pulmonary endarterectomy surgery.

Charles Haworth is the Clinical Director of Thoracic Services at Papworth.

John Dunning is a consultant surgeon at Papworth, specialising in cardiothoracic surgery and cardiopulmonary transplantation.

Stephen Bridge, the Papworth Chief Executive Officer, the second-longest serving CEO in the NHS.

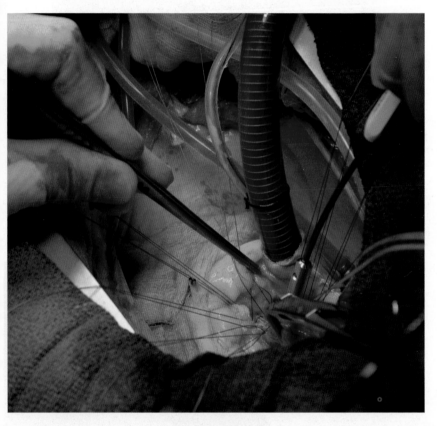

A lung operation.

Steven Tsui, a consultant surgeon at Papworth, specialises in cardiothoracic surgery and transplantation.

Samer Nashef, a consultant surgeon at Papworth, has led an international project for measuring the quality of surgical treatment (EuroSCORE).

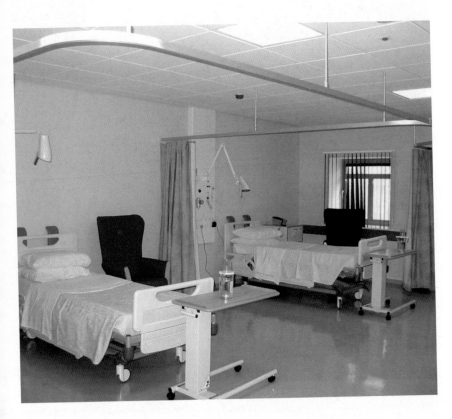

A ward in the RSSC department in Papworth.

Dr Bob Verney was the first radiologist to undertake successful percutaneous needle biopsy of the lungs.

Ellen Kemp worked at Papworth for 26 years from 1977 and set the high standard of nursing for which Papworth Hospital is known.

Roger Hall, the current Medical Director of Papworth.

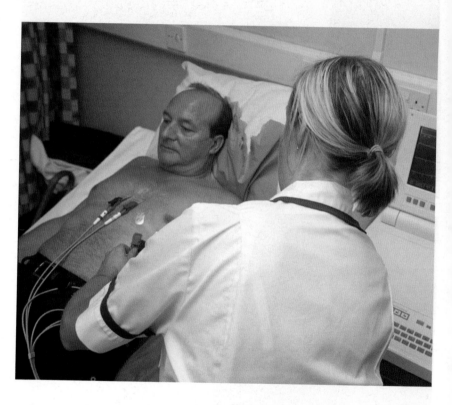

Nursing care.

Peter Schofield, a consultant
cardiologist at Papworth.

Stephen Large specialises in
heart failure surgery, upset heart
rhythms and reconstruction of
abnormalities of the heart and
thoracic aorta.

Andrew Grace, a consultant cardiologist.

Simon Fynn, Clinical Director for Cardiology at Papworth.

Josie Rudman is Director of Nursing.

Sarah Clarke is a consultant cardiologist.

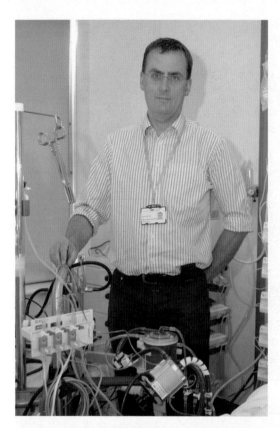

Alain Vuylsteke specialises in extracorporeal membrane oxygenation (ECMO) and pulmonary endarterectomy.

Elizabeth Horne is Director of Human Resources.

Claire Tripp is Director of Operations.

View from the north west of the new Papworth at Addenbrooke's in Cambridge.

Artist's impression of the new Papworth Hospital to be opened in 2018.

'Mr Christopher Parish, Mr B B Milstein, Mr T A English, Mr R Cory Pierce, Mr J Wallwork, Mr C M McGregor, Dr G I Verney, Dr C D R Flower, Dr J M Collis, Dr D W Bethune, Dr R Latimer and Dr J Hardy.'

On Tuesday 8th June 1982 I recovered consciousness in the Intensive Care Unit and the nurse immediately came to attend to me. She said 'Thanks for doing everything I asked you to do. Everything went perfectly, you were the perfect patient.' I was not very conscious so it must have been the training I had over the weekend. I was so pleased it had all gone so well.

I had the stomach tube removed from my mouth without any discomfort. Then the nurse showed me a valve like the one implanted in me.

I was taken back to the ward to the corner bed and not to the one behind the door. I did not feel severe pain – just some discomfort groaning even during physiotherapy. In due course the injection needle in my neck, the two tubes in my chest and the cannula in my left arm were removed. By night time I managed to pull myself upright using the rope and I was able to walk to the toilet to use the jar as everything going in and coming out of my body was being checked.

I was being encouraged to drink a lot, tea and glasses of orange juice, I vaguely remembered having some dinner as well as evening tea. The evening pills trolley came and I started taking the pills: 2 slow K, 1 furosemide (40mg), 1 digoxin (0.25mg), and warfarin.

On Wednesday 9th – I did not note the exact time when – I started making more bed ropes from ropes in the sluice room and those from Felixstowe Docks but it was as soon as I was able to. I cut the ropes into 9ft lengths, made a loop one end and a dog's tail at the other to loop onto the bottom bedrail, and tied knots at intervals to help patients get a good grip without the rope slipping through their fingers and jarring their body. Nurses brought other patients to see me working to encourage their recovery. Dennis Day was one of these and we kept in touch for many years – I visited him at Hitchin several times.

When I finished making the ropes on the 13th of June, the day my stitches came out, the nurses got me on to knitting woollen squares for a blanket. My family and I finished making one at home with a red heart and '7th June 1982' at its centre. We took it to the Papworth Hospital fête on Saturday 26th June.

I was still having my morning and evening tablets. My discharge day was on Tuesday 15th June. I was taken to see 19-year-old Tracy in the women's ward as she was terrified of her operation, and I hope I managed to ease her worries. I chatted with the lady in the next bed too. Mr Glennie arrived that day. Mr Horace Simpson (Sam) from Peterborough and Mr Somers from Ipswich are others I met at Papworth earlier. My memory is not as good as it was.

A friend drove my wife and me home to Felixstowe. He wore lead boots and said he was frightened I might collapse on him so he sped us home – safely may I add.

I returned with my family to the hospital fête on 26th of June. My wife had arranged with Sister Barker to help at the fête. We gave the woollen blanket to Sister Barker and Mrs Linda Hart's stall, but bought it back again for £20. Mrs Hart had been very kind to me during my time in Papworth.

I bought several paintings at the hospital's annual fêtes. One of them is a View from the Bubble by Mr A Barlow 1979.

I was put in touch with Mr Des Fox, Chairman of the local BCPA Zipper Club, visited him at his home in Elmswell and joined it then. Now it is 30 years on.

Putting patients at the heart

In 2009, Celia Hyde, a senior nurse at Papworth, wrote an article in the *Nursing Times*, describing her work at the hospital. *Inter alia*, she said:

Putting patients at the heart of care delivery is key to nurse leadership

Cardiothoracic transplantation is celebrating an import-ant milestone this year. At Papworth Hospital 25 years ago, Professor John Wallwork carried out Europe's first successful heart and lung transplant. I was fortunate to be a member of the nursing team in theatre that day, as an enrolled nurse who had been working just two years. Professional development opportunities have enabled me to develop as a practitioner as the transplant service has developed and grown.

In its early days the service had just two operating theatres and used temporary buildings for outpatients. Over the last quarter of a century it has grown and developed, and now uses five operating theatres, has a purpose built transplant outpatient department, a multi-disciplinary team and a well-deserved international reputation for the high quality of care it offers to the 65 new transplant recipients each year.

In terms of my own professional development, I had a clear desire to become a registered nurse, but the exams stood in my way. Not much of an obstacle, one might have thought, but a mountain to someone with dyslexia. However, my experience demonstrates that it is possible to progress up the career ladder with determination and support.

After nine years of working in theatre, I decided to try my exams again. The hospital's education department supported me throughout the process and I was allowed to move from operating theatres to the transplant out-patient service, which enabled me to concentrate on my studies. All this support paid off and I sat and passed my finals in early 1994.

By the end of that year I had been promoted to senior staff nurse in the transplant outpatient department, where I still work today. With the hospital's support, I went on to complete my diploma and then my degree. By August 2000, I was the sister in the transplant unit and just eight years later, I was appointed matron for the transplant service.

My growth has been mirrored by that of Papworth Hospital and its transplant service. We now look after 815 post-transplant patients in our clinic, and I am pleased to say that I know them all by name and they know me.

When I first joined the unit in 1991, the clinic list for the whole week was on one side of A4. Now the list is a full page each day.

As with all growth and development, it is important to remain focused on the main objective and, in both my case and that of the transplant service, it was about maintaining and improving quality. For me, professional development is not about the next job title; it is about learning new skills that will help me to provide an even better service to patients.

Just like the transplant service, I always make sure that regardless of my title, the patients I have the privilege of looking after remain at the centre of all I do.

So this year I am celebrating the success of what was achieved 25 years ago and every day since, and the opportunities I have been given to flourish.

The high standard of nursing has been a feature of Papworth Hospital, especially since the arrival of Ellen Kemp in May 1977. She was the Director of Nursing at Papworth and was closely involved in developing the professional standards of nursing of which the hospital can be justly proud.

Here are the views of some nurses, all of whom have served at Papworth for many years.

Maureen King came to Papworth from Addenbrooke's in 1985 at the behest of Ben Milstein and immediately found that being at Papworth was like being part of a family and that checking of patients was carried out in a very structured way.

Donna Ward came to Papworth in 1984 and said she felt fully included and part of the team immediately: 'Everyone is involved and the patients and relatives loved coming back to the garden parties and fêtes we organised.'

Hazel Farren, who came to Papworth in 1982 from the London Hospital, said that the family atmosphere at Papworth was very unusual and that the Senior Nurse, Ellen Kemp, was lovely to everyone, whether staff or patients, and that the surgeons trusted the nurses completely.

Natalie Doughty, who trained in oncology at the Leicester Hospital, came to Papworth in 1985 and became a specialist nurse concentrating on pulmonary thrombo-endarterectomy. She agrees with the other nurses that Papworth has a deserved reputation for almost unrivalled patient care and service.

This is what Papworth Hospital justifiably says about itself:

Papworth People

We achieve our success through the professionalism and commitment of our excellent staff. Papworth Hospital was named as a top healthcare employer in the Healthcare 100 Awards and was the first NHS hospital in England to win an award for looking after the health and wellbeing of its staff.

It is the people who make Papworth Hospital what it is and we are extremely proud of the achievements of our staff. It is their dedication, hard work and commitment that ensures we are able to give patients, their family and friends the best care and attention possible.

And here is what other people have said recently:

'My wife & I attended Papworth yesterday for her 3 month check-up in Thoracic Outpatients. It never ceases to amaze me, that whenever we attend the hospital, the staff are so cheerful and friendly, and although we cannot speak for them, they always appear to be happy & enjoying their jobs. Compared to other hospitals in the area, there always seems to be an air of calm serenity about the place, no hustle or bustle, just total efficiency. For us who are regular visitors, it's nice to see familiar faces. See you all again in October, and as ever a "big thank you" for your courtesy and consideration.'

'I would like to take this opportunity to express my gratitude to all staff encountered during my three day visits, the last visit being for an angiogram. Staff were so professional, understanding, courteous and a pleasure to be with at all times. The day ward was clean and had a delightful atmosphere. I will need to return for a heart bypass and have total confidence that I will receive the best possible care in this hospital. I just wish to convey my appreciation to all involved.'

Here is what a patient said about an overnight stay at the RSSC:

I had an overnight stay at Papworth Sleep clinic for tests on sleep apnoea and respiratory failure. I have been to Papworth for a few day clinics over the same issue and have always found them to be excellent, however the night study and overnight stay took it to a different league of care. For the record, I hate hospitals. I feel trapped, enclosed and generally really dislike them. The thought of staying overnight for me is torture. Anyway, daytime was fine for me, had various tests all of which were positive. The staff made me feel welcome. After a short wait I was told what was happening. Ward notes and consultant notes varied a bit to start with but this was sorted quickly so I knew what was going on. Unfortunately as the night came closer I started to become panicked. I wanted to discharge myself. My wife was unable to talk me around but as the night time beeps and machines come alive things got worse for me. My wife went to talk to the charge nurse who quickly came over to reassure me but at the same time said they were supportive of any decision I made. Of course they talked me around on medical advice and I remained for the night. The night time was unpleasant as it was noisy and I struggled to sleep but I had a good six hours. Through the night I wore a cpap [continuous positive airway pressure] machine for the first time which made things a bit worse, however the staff were really supportive and helpful in many areas of getting the machine right. The food was rather nice, in fact the tomato soup was some of the best I have ever tried. Because of my displeasure of hospitals my wife was told she could stay as long as she needed even if this meant she was there until I went asleep, which was over and above. Anyway I should not go on, a really special place. Food hot and tasty. Staff supportive and friendly, expert care and treatment.

This is what others had to say about the wonderful service and atmosphere at Papworth:

My husband was taken ill a month ago. He had complete heart block pulse measurement of only 30, then decreasing to a low of 19.

The ambulance crew that attended were wonderful, and after a blue light dash to Addenbrooke's, followed by the same to Papworth, he was taken to Varrier-Jones and a pacemaker was quickly inserted.

The hospital and all the staff gave excellent care. There is no aspect of this hospital that can be faulted.

All in all I can only thank everyone involved in his care. Also they looked after me and our relatives, I was able to stay in the hospital with him which was very much appreciated.

I have no hesitation in recommending this hospital most highly.

Thank you everyone so much.

Such a happy place
Yesterday my wife went for her quarterly check up in the Thoracic dept. She was seen within an hour of her appointment time, unusual in hospitals in this day and age. When we went to book her next appointment, we were given the choice of time convenient to us (we have to drive some 20 miles to get to the hospital), so this is a great help. But apart from the great care and consideration shown to us, is the apparent happiness of all the staff, we have never seen a member of staff with a 'long' face or miserable. We have visited the hospital on

a number of occasions, and yet the atmosphere is always the same, one of total control and efficiency, and although no one likes to visit hospitals , as a general rule of thumb, Papworth's staff make it a visit not to be missed. A big thanks, yet again to all the staff. We look forward to seeing you all again in June.

Lifesaving, gold star treatment

In December I was flown in the Magpas Helicopter to Papworth Hospital from south Lincolnshire suffering a heart attack.

Nobody could have been more surprised than me that I was having a heart attack ... a heart attack? Me? Non-smoker, fit, good diet, exercise. Seems blood clots have no respect!

What followed still amazes me today as I sit here at my computer writing this ...

Paramedic, Ambulance, Helicopter, Ambulance, Theatre, HDU – and all within 2 hours or so. Who can't fail to be impressed with such a chain of events? Amazing, awesome and every other word that can best describe the lifesaving, gold star treatment I received.

Well, I appear to be well on the mend thanks in no small way to the prompt, timely and well co-ordinated intervention by all involved.

I was mightily impressed at the time and have continued to reflect on my good fortune ever since and continue to do so.

My heartfelt (no pun intended) thanks go to everyone involved in my care and treatment.

No criticism of the NHS here, it's thanks to their co-ordination, professionalism and expertise that I'm writing this at all!

In the spring of 2015, Jo-Anne Fowles, ECMO Lead/CCA Matron at Papworth, won the Teva Innovations in the Respiratory category of the Nursing Standard Nurse Awards for her achievements in improving patient care at Papworth.

Papworth village

Papworth Hospital is very fortunate to have the support of many households in the village that offer accommodation to patients and relatives who need to stay at times near the hospital or who have repeat out-patient visits and travel from all over the country.

Over the years strong ties have been established and they have offered a great service to the patients, relatives and the hospital. This was originally set up for the transplantation patients by Virginia O'Brien, who was the hospital social worker for most of the 1980s.

Although the hospital now has hostel facilities in the village for some patients, this is a valuable service which will be missed when the hospital relocates to the Biomedical Campus in Cambridge.

Chapter 10

THE MOVE TO CAMBRIDGE

Papworth in the 1990s
'Papworth was quite temporary'
'Will bring benefits to patients'
Research, development and education

Papworth in the 1990s

As we have seen, the possible move of Papworth to join Addenbrooke's in Cambridge was constantly discussed and reviewed and, in 1998, a paper by Dr Ron Zimmern, Director of Public Health for Cambridge and Huntingdon Health Authority, and Stephen Bridge, Chief Executive, Papworth Hospital, set out to review the various options for the future development of specialist cardiothoracic facilities to meet service needs in the Eastern Region.

It showed, *inter alia*, that Papworth had grown considerably in the previous decade and where it was in its services and treatments:

Finished consultant episodes	4,258 to 13,044
Out-patients	3,100 to 11,361
Beds	125 to 206
Consultant staff	13 to 34
Visiting cardiologists	3 to 9
Operations	620 to 1,548
Research staff	7 to 38
Annual budget	£9m to £36m

The practice of thoracic medicine at Papworth had changed in the 1990s. By the end of the decade, it was providing a specialist service for general chest medicine and several other specific areas. The specialist areas firmly established were:

A Respiratory Sleep and Support Centre
An adolescent and young adult Cystic Fibrosis Centre

A rapid screening and treatment unit for the care of
   lung cancer patients
A Pulmonary Hypertension Unit
An Immunology Unit with a Host Defence Team

These required the presence of on-site specialist radiology, pathology and respiratory physiology services, which
had been enhanced significantly during the previous
five years. There were close links with service provision
at Addenbrooke's, Hinchingbrooke and West Suffolk
Hospitals, where the chest physicians were intimately
involved in the management of a wide spectrum of respiratory disease, and referred to Papworth complex problems
which required its specialist expertise and facilities. These
patients required either (a) investigations such as transbronchial or needle biopsies or (b) procedures such as bronchial
stenting or pulmonary artery embolisation.

'Papworth was quite temporary'
In 2014 it was finally decided that Papworth Hospital
would join Addenbrooke's Hospital on the Cambridge
Biomedical Campus. When I began the research for this
book I thought discussions about this move had been
going on for ten years. I was soon informed it was more
like 30 years, and finally Julia Fleming, widow of Hugh
Fleming, informed me that actually it was 55 years. Hugh
Fleming remembered that:

Right from the beginning [1959] we understood that our
stay at Papworth was quite temporary and that before

long we would be moved into the new Addenbrooke's Hospital site. I well remember that staff appointed as early as 1961 had this explained to them at interview. Julia has vivid memories of this and, on her appointment, was told that within a year or two she would be back working at Addenbrooke's in Cambridge. Because of this uncertainty no capital development was ever made at Papworth in my time and indeed the authorities were very unwilling to spend even minimal amounts of money on keeping up the repair of the place. In the early years Papworth was under the Regional Health Authority who regarded cardiology and thoracic surgery as jewels in their crown. Addenbrooke's Hospital under its Board of Governors came under quite a different establishment and there was considerable jealousy between these two bodies, which inhibited any constructive discussion about amalgamation.

'Will bring benefits to patients'

Finally, in 2010, it was looking as though the move was going to happen and John Wallwork, who became Chairman of the Board of Papworth Hospital NHS Trust, was absolutely determined that the move should happen. He was able to tell *Circulation*, the journal of the American Heart Association:

The new Papworth will be a 21st-century centre for treating heart and lung disease. It will include a state-of the-art teaching hospital capable of delivering the ser- vices expected from an internationally recognised centre of specialist care and a unique research facility where the researchers of the University of Cambridge and the clinicians of Papworth can work together to find new ways to treat and cure cardiothoracic diseases. This meeting of clinicians and researchers under one roof will provide the ideal opportunity for academic synergy, growth and innovation.

In December 2013 it was announced that 'One of the largest specialist heart and lung hospitals is to move to a new £165m building on the Cambridge Biomedical Campus'.

By this time Papworth Hospital was treating more than 23,700 in-patients and day cases plus nearly 65,000 out-patients a year. Chief Executive, Stephen Bridge, said that the move would create jobs and 'attract leading clinicians and researchers to Cambridge'.

However, now that it had Department of Health approval, the project had to go for consideration by HM Treasury. On 14 February 2014 *The Guardian* wrote:

The future of the world-renowned Papworth hospital is in doubt because it is being prevented by the Treasury from moving to a new centre of medical excellence in Cambridge.

Instead of consolidating its reputation as a pioneering heart and lung hospital at the forefront of medical innovation, Papworth may instead be forced into a shotgun partnership with the NHS's most loss-making foundation trust.

Stephen Bridge, Chief Executive of Papworth – scene of the UK's first heart transplant and a host of other medical breakthroughs – told *The Guardian* that his hospital may become a casualty of 'NHS politics' and is 'exasperated' at the Treasury's eleventh-hour intervention.

'We could be forever caught up in NHS politics, get bogged down and be left with an uncertain future,' said Bridge.

Papworth has had to put on hold its long-planned transfer to a state-of-the-art site outside Cambridge as a result of the Treasury's intervention, despite the move having widespread support in the NHS and academia and from the Department of Health (DH).

The specialist heart and lung hospital may now have to instead move some or all of its services, including cardiac surgery and world-leading transplantation, to Peterborough as part of a rescue plan for Peterborough city hospital.

Peterborough and Stamford NHS Foundation Trust, which runs it, is losing millions of pounds a month, has received £44m in emergency funding from the DH to continue operating and was last year declared 'not financially sustainable' by the NHS's economic regulator Monitor.

Papworth, based 12 miles west of Cambridge, has been planning for 10 years to leave its ageing site and relocate to a new £160m 310-bed hospital in the Cambridge Biomedical Campus, a huge new medical and science park next to the city's Addenbrooke's hospital, which will ultimately employ 30,000 people and be one of the world's biggest centres of research and treatment.

The move is so advanced that Papworth has already appointed construction firm Skanska to build its new facility. The DH approved the move last October and has also arranged £70m in low-interest loans to help Papworth meet the £160m overall cost. The hospital has to borrow the remaining £90m from banks under the private finance initiative (PFI), with that deal needing the Treasury's approval.

But in an unexpected intervention, the Treasury has ordered Monitor to undertake two reviews, which will take several months to complete, before it will approve any move by Papworth.

The first is a review of Papworth's finances – the third such exercise in three years – which it has commissioned despite Papworth being one of the NHS's strongest performers financially and the two previous reviews having raised no concerns.

The other, a short clinical review being undertaken by an independent leading NHS doctor, is examining the 'arguments for and against proposals to locate the facility as planned next to Addenbrooke's hospital as well as a clinical review of the feasibility of the utilisation of any excess capacity at Peterborough.' The Peterborough hospital, which is struggling to repay a controversial PFI debt, has vacant space which Papworth may help to fill.

The Treasury's move has raised concerns that Papworth's key role in the new biomedical campus, which will see its experts pursue major innovations in treatment for a range of diseases, may be sacrificed because of a desire to improve the finances of Peterborough hospital.

Bridge said he was 'disappointed and exasperated' that 'the Peterborough option' had been resurrected by the Treasury, even though a report by Monitor last September ruled it out. Patients would benefit from Papworth going to Cambridge because it could then 'develop market-leading specialist services for the NHS in one place', the regulator concluded.

Patients may lose out and the Papworth trust's future be in question if some or all its services and 2,000 staff end up going to Peterborough rather than Cambridge, he added.

'Despite providing very detailed financial and clinical evidence as to why Papworth should move to Cambridge, we were informed by the Department of Health [in December] that we now have to answer these questions, including about why some of our work couldn't move to Peterborough,' Bridge said.

'I'm exasperated as only in May last year and again in September last year I was officially told that there was no longer any suggestion that any of Papworth's services should move to Peterborough hospital.'

The DH told Papworth about the Treasury-ordered reviews barely two months after health minister Earl Howe had approved the move.

Bridge added: 'The clinical reasons for us moving to Cambridge are overwhelming. We do heart and lung transplants and would be next door to Addenbrooke's, which does liver and kidney transplants. We would create a world-leading solid organ transplant centre.'

He is worried that, without final approval soon for the move to Cambridge, Papworth could be targeted under DH plans currently going through parliament to give government-appointed special administrators the power to push through changes at profitable trusts situated near hospitals which have hit major financial problems, such as Peterborough.

NHS England, Cambridge University and major medical charities such as the British Heart Foundation and Cystic Fibrosis Trust strongly back Papworth moving to Cambridge.

Julian Huppert, the Liberal Democrat MP for Cambridge, warned that forcing Papworth to share with Peterborough city hospital was not sensible clinically and would ultimately cost more money.

'The well-known problems of PFI contracts that the last government was so keen on should not cause worse treatment now for another hospital. They should not force Papworth to go to the wrong place simply to patch up other problems. It doesn't make sense to spend more money on a worse outcome simply because of previous problems at Peterborough that are entirely separate,' Huppert said.

'Papworth moving to the Addenbrooke's site is the right thing clinically for the patient and the right thing in terms of research and developing new treatments,' added Huppert, a scientist.

The Treasury and DH declined to answer questions put to them about their involvement with Papworth and instead issued a joint statement through a government spokesman.

He insisted that 'the Department of Health is still considering the [Papworth] trust's business case', even though it signed that off four months ago.

'A joint decision with the Treasury will be made soon. As is normal for major projects such as this one, the Department and the Treasury, drawing on the expertise of Monitor, would expect assurance around the afford-ability of the scheme and whether it represents value for money for the taxpayer,' he added.

Monitor is looking for 'assurance' from the reviews that 'the proposed future location of Papworth hospital … will be sustainable, is clinically and financially appro-priate, and will provide good value for money for the taxpayer.' The huge task in moving is illustrated by the activity of Papworth in 2013/14.

Papworth Hospital Activity in 2013/14:
- 886 cardiac ablations (£2,939,221)
- 891 CABG (£8,605,097)
- 602 valve surgeries (£7,022,720)
- 81 transplants (£7,503,768.04)
- 162 PTE (£5,323,200)
- 23 VADs – long- and short-term (£2,789,919)
- 664 primary percutaneous coronary intervention (PPCI) – (£3,438,341)
- 89 thoracic surgeries (£176,358)

Papworth Hospital continues to perform above the national targets set by Monitor:

- 18 weeks RTT (Regional Transfusion Team) for admitted patients: 92 per cent (>90 per cent national target)
- 18 weeks RTT for non-admitted patients: 97.9 per cent (>95 per cent)
- Cancer: 31-day diagnosis to treatment: 98.7 per cent (96 per cent)
- Cancer: 31-day wait for second and subsequent treatment: 100 per cent (94 per cent)

On 23 December 2014 it was announced that land had been bought on the Cambridge Biomedical Campus in preparation for building to begin early in 2015. The area was over seven acres in size and located on the centre of the campus. Stephen Bridge said:

The Trust is developing its plans for a £165 million state-of-the-art Papworth Hospital on the Cambridge Biomedical Campus. The co-location of Papworth Hospital with the other organisations on the Campus will bring benefits to patients as they will have immediate access to a range of services and also bring opportunities in terms of research and education on which the treatments of tomorrow will be based. The Trust is working with the two consortia which have progressed through the earlier stages of the bidding process, to further develop their bids, before a preferred bidder is selected and a contract signed. The new hospital is expected to be completed in 2018.

Research, development and education

Ever since its beginnings, with the work of Varrier-Jones, Papworth has had a major interest in developing new therapies through careful research and evaluation and the subsequent dissemination of this knowledge by teaching and training all grades of healthcare professionals from the UK and worldwide.

Papworth has had considerable influence in improving patient care in almost every continent from all the specialised areas that have been established and developed at the hospital.

The three elements that form the tri-partite mission – patient care (service)/research and development/education and training – have always been at the forefront of Papworth's thinking, but at times they have not been afforded attention in equal measure. Over the years, and particularly more recently, the pressure from the NHS to deliver the service needs of the patients has led to research and development, and to a lesser extent education, not being given the full attention they need.

The isolation of the hospital has also limited the scope of research and as mentioned below has been for many years a major driver towards the move into Cambridge.

This is not to say that Papworth has not been successful in the areas in which it excels. It has led in many fields of heart and lung medicine and surgery, but the majority of that work has been confined to what is now called translational research, in the form of clinical trials and development of novel techniques in patient care. However, there are established links with more basic science in the

Medical School and the wider University in Cambridge that have been very productive. The full potential of these links has yet to be seen, as is discussed below.

The formal R&D department was established on the back of an independent review into the cost and benefits of heart transplantation conducted in the early 1980s by Martin Buxton, a health economist from Brunel University, and Noreen Caine from the department of Community Medicine in Cambridge. She became the first director of the R&D department at Papworth and established links with Health Enterprise East, which was housed at Papworth and was responsible for the opening of a biomedical incubator (nothing to do with babies!) to help small and evolving companies in the biomedical field to grow.

One of the strengths of the R&D department was the appointment of Linda Sharples, as a member of the renowned MRC biostatistics unit in the University, to be the biostatistician at Papworth. She brought a vigour and credibility to the data that the hospital researches produced and enhanced the reputation of its clinical research outcomes.

However, it has for many years been clear that Papworth alone could not attract research investment from the major research establishments such as the British Heart Foundation and the MRC from a position of relative isolation without forming stronger and lasting alliances with the Medical School in Cambridge.

This was, with other elements, a major factor in the need to move the hospital closer to Addenbrooke's Hospital. Now that the move onto the Biomedical Campus in

Cambridge is a reality, the development of a world-famous cardiothoracic research and education institute is feasible and no longer an unattainable goal.

This move should allow the excellence in science that exists already through the proximity to the new hospital to release fully the potential to lead heart and lung investigation for the benefit of patients worldwide.

Education and specialist training, particularly for postgraduate doctors, nurses and other professional groups, has always been strong at Papworth Hospital. It has established a reputation for providing high-quality teaching and this is reflected in the intense competition for official training programmes run at the hospital for national recognition.

In attracting some of the brightest and the best, Papworth's influence on a career has been felt not just by individuals but by the places they have gone on to work, and where in many cases they have developed their own outstanding units.

The hospital, as a result of its reputation, has also seen many healthcare professionals from abroad come for highly specialised training in all departments of the hospital who have influenced patient care in countries around the world – in Asia, North and South America, the Middle East and closer to home in Europe. They have not only taken the formal aspects of their training home but also the culture and ethos of the hospital, on which patients and staff often comment. These are important attributes to maintain when the research and education institute moves adjacent to the new hospital.

And it looks as though, finally, in 2015, Papworth Hospital WILL be moved to a site in Cambridge alongside Addenbrooke's Hospital.

Papworth Hospital Chairman, Professor John Wallwork, was able to announce:

We are delighted to hear that Danny Alexander MP and George Osborne [Chancellor of the Exchequer] have signed off the business case for the New Papworth Hospital project, following Mr Osborne's pledge of personal support for the project.

For many years we have been convinced that the right place for this world class institution to provide high-quality services for patients with heart and lung conditions from across the countryside is on the Cambridge Biomedical Campus. We now look forward to putting that vision into reality.

John Wallwork went on to give great credit to the Chief Executive, Stephen Bridge, who he said had run a very stable administration and had been good at seizing opportunities and adapting to new regulations. His management had been totally consistent and he had enabled Papworth to grow and achieve the very high quality which was noted in the Report of the Care Quality Commission which said:

Papworth NHS Foundation Trust provides the UK's largest specialist cardiothoracic hospital and the country's main heart and lung transplant centre. The trust treats over 23,700 inpatient and day cases and provides over 124,066 outpatient appointments each year.

Services are internationally recognised and include cardiology, respiratory medicine, and cardiothoracic surgery and transplantation. Papworth Hospital is a regional centre for the diagnosis and treatment of cardiothoracic disease, and a national centre for a range of specialist services, including pulmonary endarterectomy. It is one of the first centres in Europe to offer transcatheter aortic valve implantation (TAVI).

Papworth Hospital has the largest respiratory support and sleep centre in the UK.

We carried out this inspection as part of our comprehensive inspection programme.

We carried out an announced inspection of the hospital on 3 and 4 December 2014, and an unannounced inspection on 14 December. We looked at all the inpatient services, including the Progressive Care Unit, and the outpatients department.

Our key findings were:

Overall we found that the trust provided highly effective care with outcomes comparable with or above expected standards. The service was delivered by highly skilled, committed, caring staff and patients were overwhelmingly positive about the care they received at the hospital. We rated both the effective and the caring domains as outstanding.

There were elements of the well led domain that were very good, particularly in relation to the comprehensive research and development programme that encouraged service development and innovation for the benefit of patients. There was a very positive culture in the trust. Staff were very proud of the work they did and very proud of the trust. They were aware of the trust's positive reputation and worked hard to maintain and enhance it.

Nurse staffing

Care and treatment were delivered by committed and caring nursing staff who worked well together for the benefit of patients. Nurse staffing levels were calculated using a recognised dependency tool and there were sufficient numbers of skilled and suitably qualified nurses to meet the needs of patients.

Medical staffing

Care and treatment were delivered by highly skilled and committed medical staff. There were excellent examples of senior medical staff supporting development and innovation in cardiothoracic services nationally and internationally. There was a good consultant presence throughout the wards, providing care to patients seven days a week.

A 'consultant of the week' system had recently been initiated in medicine and was working well. A comprehensive handover took place from one consultant to another. Patients received high-quality care and treatment and were exceptionally complimentary about the medical staff in the trust.

Junior medical staff we spoke with felt well supported

in their roles by senior medical staff and did not feel their workload was excessive. Findings from the General Medical Council Survey 2014 supported this.

Leadership of the trust

There was strong leadership and good management support for staff from their line managers. Staff felt supported and valued. The Executive team and the Chairman were visible and accessible to staff at trust level and supported the delivery of high-quality care, learning and innovation.

The trust had provided leadership development programmes including a development programme for nursing staff at bands 5 and 6. The leadership programmes were evaluated well by staff, who felt it supported their professional development.

There were some very positive role models for staff at service and trust level. There was strong evidence of staff in all disciplines that were very focused and committed to developing and improving services that would improve clinical outcomes, longevity and quality of life for patients in their care.

Culture within the trust

There was a very positive culture in the trust. Staff were very proud of the work they did and very proud of the trust. They were aware of the trust's positive reputation and worked hard to maintain and enhance that reputation through a commitment to continuous improvement and innovation.

Fit and proper persons

The trust had robust recruitment policies and proce-dures in place for recruiting its directors and senior team. Directors were appropriately vetted and checked before appointment.

Public and staff engagement

The trust was proactive in securing patient feedback and used it effectively to improve patients' experience. Staff routinely engaged with patients and their rela-tives to seek their views about their experiences at the trust.

The trust was highly regarded in the local area and enjoyed good support from local residents, who often offered visitors and patients affordable accommodation within the village of Papworth Everard.

Staff received communications in a variety of ways such as newsletters, emails, briefing documents and meetings. All staff were aware of the plans for the new hospital and were positive about the opportunities this would bring for the further development and expansion of services.

Wallwork emphasised Stephen Bridge's 'vast knowledge of how everything works' and that he had been tenacious about moving to Addenbrooke's, especially in the last eleven years.

There had been considerable difficulty in securing final Treasury approval for the move but at least the support of the Prime Minister was secured:

HOUSE OF COMMONS
LONDON SWIA 0AA

Professor A.R. Michell
Tuesday, 25th March 2014.
Ref: DC/js/M

Dear Professor Michell,
Thank you for your recent letter about the proposed move of Papworth Hospital.

I can appreciate your desire to see Papworth move to Addenbrooke's and do take on board the points you make about the clinical benefits that such a move would bring. I have therefore written to Earl Howe, Parliamentary Under-Secretary of State for Quality at the Department of Health, to ensure that your concerns can be understood at the highest possible level.

As soon as I receive his reply, I will be back in touch with you. Thank you again for taking the time and trouble to write to me.

Let us see what he says.

Yours sincerely,
David Cameron

The move was certainly going to be a formidable operation. By the end of 2014, Papworth Hospital had about 1,800 staff in the following groups:

Nursing 43 per cent
Allied healthcare professionals (pharmacists, dieticians, physiotherapists) 6 per cent

Professional and scientific 4 per cent
Ancillary / Estates 4 per cent
Bank staff 7 per cent
Medical 9 per cent
Technicians 6 per cent
Senior managers 2 per cent
Administration (clinical support staff, e.g. ward clerks,
    medical secretaries) 19 per cent

275 beds, including 39 intensive care beds
Five operating theatres
Five cardiac catheterisation laboratories

£130 million turnover
86 per cent elective activity

The growth since 1982 had been considerable. Then there were three surgeons. By 2014 there were fourteen, assisted by 20 anaesthetists. 23,820 in-patient and day cases and 72,891 out-patients were treated in 2014.

On 18 March 2015 a reception was held at St James's Palace, hosted by HRH the Duchess of Gloucester, a great supporter of Papworth. She said:

As Patron of Papworth Hospital NHS Foundation Trust, I am delighted to support its innovative and cutting-edge work. This evening is the perfect occasion to showcase Papworth Hospital's remarkable achievements, as well as looking to its future of innovation and collaboration on the Cambridge biomedical campus.

Regardless of location, though, it is the people behind Papworth Hospital that maintain the high-quality standards of care that patients have come to expect. The hospital benefits from a hugely dedicated team of consultants, physicians, surgeons, nursing staff and support services and many more. Together they provide life-changing, and in some cases lifelong, care for people who would otherwise struggle with their day-to-day lives due to debilitating cardiothoracic conditions.

John Wallwork responded:

Innovation and collaboration are two of the most fundamental factors in moving medicine forward and have been the cornerstone by which Papworth Hospital clinicians, nurses and supporting medical teams have provided world-class care to our patients over the decades.

The long-awaited move of Papworth Hospital to the Cambridge biomedical campus will give a once in a lifetime opportunity to develop a world-class research institute for heart and lung disease.

As part of Papworth Hospital's vision for the future and in order to continue to deliver cutting-edge cardiothoracic medicine and technology, we must invest in research.

Our ambition is to lead rather than follow and to provide tomorrow's medicine today, not today's medicine tomorrow.

A booklet issued to all attendees at the reception at St James's Palace explained the new Papworth Hospital's ambitions under the heading:

THE FUTURE OF INNOVATION

Heart and Lung Research and Education Institute

Diseases of the heart and lung are amongst the biggest killers worldwide. Despite a growing awareness of risk factors, such as smoking and poor diet, and the availability of some treatments, the prevalence of such diseases is increasing. There is an urgent need for a greater understanding of the causes of these diseases and to take new treatments from bench to bedside.

Fundraising is now underway to support a major expansion of cardio-respiratory research in Cambridge, with the creation of a new world-leading Heart and Lung Research Institute jointly established by Papworth Hospital and the University of Cambridge, to sit alongside the new Papworth Hospital on the Cambridge Biomedical Campus.

The Institute will provide a cutting-edge environment for genetics, laboratory and population sciences to collaborate with clinical medicine. Together, we aim to tackle the big challenges in heart and lung disease facing our population now and in the future. The Institute will also provide a facility to train and educate the next generation of outstanding scientists and clinicians.

BIBLIOGRAPHY

Papers of a Pioneer, Sir Pendrill Varrier-Jones, Hutchinson
    & Co., 1943

The Papworth Families, E.M. Brieger, William Heinemann, 1944

Follow Your Star, Terence English, AuthorHouse, 2011

On the Road, Rowland Parker, Pendragon Press, 1977

Heart and Heart–Lung Transplantation, John Wallwork,
    Sanders, 1989

Development of Cardiothoracic Surgery at Papworth Hospital,
    B.B. Milstein, Papworth Hospital, 1997

Papworth Cardiac Unit, Hugh Fleming, Papworth Hospital, 1996

Papworth Hospital and Village Settlement, Eleanor Birks,
    Papworth Hospital, 1999

A New Beginning: Memoirs of Voluntary Worker Fred Roach,
    Papworth Hospital, 1997

The Naked Surgeon, Samer Nashef, Scribe Publications, 2015

Mitral Valve Disease, F.C. Wells, L.M. Shapiro,
    Butterworth-Heinemann, 1995

Heart Disease, John Wallwork, Rob Stepney, Wiley-Blackwell,
    1987

The Heart of Leonardo, Francis Wells, Springer-Verlag, 2013

Transplantation Immunology: Clinical and Experimental, Roy
    Calne, Oxford University Press, 1984

INDEX

acute trauma 218
Addenbrooke's Hospital 16
   and cardiac transplantation
      89–91
   oesophageal surgery 218
   Papworth Hospital move to
      site 156–7, 257, 258–66,
      268–70, 274–6
   Papworth links with 258
   pathology 189
after-care 8, 21–3, 34
Agrawal, Bobby 219
agriculture 27
Alexander, Danny 270
Allbutt, Clifford 8, 32
angina 190–1
angiography 69–70, 183
angioplasty 86–7, 190
animal organs 167
aortic aneurysm 63, 195, 216
aortic surgery 195
aortic valve replacement 191
aortic valve stenosis 196
arrhythmia 184–6
   surgery for 195
arrhythmogenic right ventricular
      cardiomyopathia (ARVC)
      169

artificial hearts *see* mechanical
   hearts
asplenia 73
atrial fibrillation 185, 195
Attlee, Clement 42

Baldwin, Stanley 17
Barber, Brenda 149–52
Barber, Samantha Jane 150, 152
Barber, Stephen 150
Barker, Sister 241, 244–5
Barlow, Andrew 98, 245
Barnard, Christiaan 87, 88, 176
Barrowmore Hall 34
Barry, Dr 239
Baxter Health Care Corporation
   165
Baxter Novacor 164
BCPA Zipper Club 245
Bennett, Julie 156
Bernhard Baron Hospital 72
Bernhard Baron Trust 15
beta blockade 231
Bethune, Don 60, 93
Bevan, Aneurin 42–6
Beveridge, William 42
Biggs, Hermann 22, 29–30
Billingham, Margaret 81, 158

Billroth, Theodore 67
Bilton, Di 213
biomedical incubator 268
BiVADs 233
Bjork Shiley aortic valve implant
   239–40
Borne, Miss K.L. 34
Bourn 3, 9, 11–13, 18
brain death
   concerns over 111–14
   defining 92
   equated to death of patient
      109–10, 117, 134–5
Bridge, Stephen 154, 211, 257,
   260–1, 263–4, 266
   Wallwork on 270, 274
British Cardiac Society 148
British Lung Foundation 212
British Medical Association 43, 45
Brock, Russell 57, 74, 79
Brompton Hospital 35, 53, 55,
   60, 74
Burnett, Pauline 105
Burt, Alan 54
Butterfield, John 96–7, 98
Buxton, Martin 268

CABG 183, 189–91, 216
Caine, Noreen 268
Calman recommendations 213
Calne, Roy
   cardiac transplantation
      investigation 57–8, 85
   and heart, lung and liver
      transplant 155
   and heart transplants 89–91,
      94–8, 118
   on *Panorama* programme 135–7
   published work 81

Cambridge Biomedical Campus
   258, 260–2, 266, 268–70, 278
Cambridge Centre for Lung
   Infection (CCLI) 211
Cambridge Evening News 100,
   117–18, 137, 138, 168–72
Cambridge Medical School 268
Cambridge News 173–6, 218–19
Cambridgeshire Tuberculosis
   After-Care Association 8, 9
Cambridgeshire Tuberculosis
   Colony 3, 9, 32
   see also Papworth Colony
Cameron, David 275
Cannon, Roberta 137
cardiac arrest 226, 227
cardiac arrhythmia 184–6
   surgery for 195
cardiac catheterisation 54–5,
   68–75, 78
cardiac clinics 63–4
cardiac imaging 186–8
Cardiac Medical Unit 50
cardiac pacemakers 73
cardiac pacing 182
Cardiac Recovery Unit 216
cardiac rejection, definition 158
cardiac resynchronisation therapy
   (CRT) 231
cardiac surgery 189–95
   early 48–9
   monitoring 207–8
      see also EuroSCORE
   operation numbers 189
   risks 61
   survival rates 204, 210–11
cardiac transplantation
   assessment for 131–4
   in critically ill patients 232

DCD heart transplantation
    173–8
demand 172–3
first three at Papworth 58,
    93–5, 97, 98
first in world 87
funding 105–6
numbers to date 106
objections 111–15, 116–21,
    122–7
    medical misgivings 123–5
    moral and scientific aspects
    125–7
    see also brain death
problems 102
support for 127–8
Urgent List 231
see also heart–lung transplants
Cardiac Unit 64
annual report (1961) 77–9
cardiology 182–8
    background 65–8
    setting up 75
cardiopulmonary bypass (CPB)
    226–7
    research 60
Care Quality Commission Report
    270–4
Cassel, Ernest 11, 32
Castle, Keith 97, 99–100, 128
Caves, Philip 127, 130, 158
Cheere, Charles Madryll 13
Cheffins, Michael 53, 60, 63
chest medicine 211–13
chronic obstructive pulmonary
    disease (COPD) 214
chronic thromboembolic
    pulmonary hypertension
    (CTEPH) 226–7, 228–9

Churchill, Winston 42
Clarke, Sarah 184
Clinical Care Area 181
clinical research 238
Cole, Dr 50
computed tomography
    angiography (CTA) 187–8
    see also CT scanning
confidence interval 202–3
consciousness, capacity for 113
'consultant of the week' system
    272
consumption see tuberculosis
Cooper, David 93
coronary artery bypass grafting
    (CABG) 183, 189–91, 216
coronary artery disease 67, 103
coronary catheterisation 186
Cory-Pearce, Richard 120
Critical Care 215–16
CT scanning 189, 218–19
CTEPH 226–7, 228–9
Cyclosporin A 124, 127, 135–6
cystic fibrosis 143, 144–5, 146,
    152, 156, 213

Davy, Humphrey 225
Day, Dennis 244
DCD heart transplantation
    173–8
    ethical considerations 177
    first at Papworth 173–6
DCD liver transplantation 176–7
DCD lung transplantation 177
DCD renal transplantation 176–7
death, defining 205–7
death for transplant purposes see
    brain death
Densem, Cameron 197

donation after brain-stem death
(DBD) 172, 174, 176, 178
Donation after Circulatory
Determined Death (DCD)
173, 176–8
see also DCD heart
transplantation
Doughty, Natalie 248
Dunning, John 226

early death 205–7
echocardiogram 186–7
ECLS 216
ECMO 215–16
education and training 269
Edwards, John 94, 150
Edwards Lifesciences 194, 196–7
Eisenmenger's syndrome 143,
144–5, 146
employment of tuberculous
24–30
English, Ian 40, 52–3, 55
English, Terence
arrival at Papworth 85–6
on assessment of patients
131–4
and first heart transplants 58,
93–8, 156
and Flower 80
foreword to Nashef book
208–10
on heart transplants 153
and mechanical heart implants
162
on organ donation 110–11
on publicity 128–30
quotes 88–9, 90–9, 101–5
and Stanford 130–1
Enham 35

European Association for
Cardio-Thoracic Surgery
198, 200
EuroSCORE 198–208, 209
EuroSCORE II 198–9, 205–7
Evans, David Wainwright 73,
89–90, 92, 111–15
on heart transplants 116–18
EVOLUTION II trial 194
extended criteria donors (ECD)
173
extracorporeal life support
(ECLS) 216
extracorporeal membrane
oxygenation (ECMO)
215–16

Farren, Hazel 248
Felixstowe 242, 244
First World War 41
Fleming, Hugh 73–7
appointment 50, 55, 63
on cardiology 182–3
and heart transplants 89, 90,
117
published work 79
quotes 64–5, 77–9, 258–9
Fleming, Julia 258–9
Florey, Howard 48
Flower, Chris 79–80
Fowler, James Kingston 32
Fowles, Jo-Anne 253
Fox, Des 245

Gamgee, Arthur 31
Gay, Alan 119, 151
Gill, Roy 60
Glennie, Mr 244
Gloucester, Duchess of 276–7

Glynn, Ian 53
Godber, George 89
Gold, Ron 69–70, 79
Goodwin, John 95–6
Gordon, William 239–45
Grace, Andrew 185
Green, Matthew 169–72
Greenberg, Martin 53, 60, 63, 71
Gregg, Duncan 51, 68–71, 73, 78
Grove, Dr 49
Groves, Edmund 50, 73

Haggar, David 241
Harefield Hospital 106, 127, 149
Harrison, Kent 40
Hart, Linda 245
Hart, Peter 241
Harvard Criteria 176
Hawthorne effect 203–4, 208
Health Enterprise East 268
Healthcare 100 Awards 248
heart bypass see coronary artery
    bypass grafting
heart disease, types 67
heart failure service 231–4
heart, lung and liver transplant
    155
heart–lung machine 57, 86, 191,
    229
    development 55
Heart–Lung Machine
    Department 59–63
Heart and Lung Research and
    Education Institute 278
heart–lung transplants 143–53
    conditions potentially suitable
    143
    controversy over 147–9
    first at Papworth 147–53

first in world 147
indications for surgery 144–6
need for 146–7
numbers to date 106
heart surgery see cardiac surgery
heart transplant see cardiac
    transplantation
Higenbottam, Tim 81, 223
Hinchingbrooke Hospital 189,
    258
Hodder, Dr 240
Hoffler, Friedrich 3
Hooley, Ernest Terah 13
hospital mortality 201–2
Howe, Earl 263, 275
Howell–Jolly bodies 72–3
Hubbard, Charles 53, 60
Humana Inc 162
Hunter, J.B. 33, 40–1
Huppert, Julian 219, 264
Hyde, Celia 245–7
hypothermia 53, 176, 226–7

idleness, enforced 24, 25
Immunology Unit 258
immunosuppression 104, 124,
    127–8, 136
innovation, future of 278
Intensive Care Cardiology 232
International Society for Heart
    and Lung Transplantation
    (ISHLT) 81, 156, 158
    grading system 158
intravascular ultrasound 187
Ipswich 49, 239
Isoniazid 41
Izukawa, Dr 79

James, Peter 58

Jamieson, Stuart 228
Johnson, Boris 42

Kemp, Ellen 247, 248
King, Maureen 247
Koch, Robert 3

Large, Stephen 172–3, 175, 176
Left Ventricular Assist Device
    164
Lillehei, C. Walton 53
Listener, on Papworth 128–35
Loder, Robert 40, 55
Lower, Richard 88
Lum, Claude 49, 59–60, 63
lung cancer 213, 217, 218
lung infections 211
lung transplants
    DCD 177
    numbers to date 106
    as unsuccessful 150
    see also heart–lung transplants
LVADs 232–3

Macleod, Iain 49–50
magnetic resonance imaging
    (MRI) 188, 189
Mary, Queen (wife of George V)
    13–14, 17
MAZE procedure 195
McHugh, Charles 93–5
McMaster, Paul 93, 96, 97
McNeil, Keith 223
measuring outcomes 198–211
mechanical hearts
    demand 165
    early experimental experience
        104
    as ethical alternative 166–8

first complete transplant at
    Papworth 168–72
first implant at Papworth
    161–6
    limitations 171–2
medical staffing 272–3
Mesobank 212
mesothelioma 211–12
Messer, Simon 174, 175
metal valves 239
Michel, Philippe 199–200
Michell, A.R. 275
Mick Knighton Mesothelioma
    Research Fund 212
Mills, Ivor 90
Milner, Frederick 13, 32
Milstein, Ben
    appointment 51, 74–5
    and cardiac transplantation
        89–90
    and closed cardiac surgery 63
    obituary 56–9
    and open-heart surgery 53–5
    operations performed 239,
        241
    and Papworth cultural ethos
        62
    on Papworth waiting lists
        137–9
    on partnership with English
        85–6
    and Radner procedure 71
    and Sochocky 52
    on Varrier-Jones 35–6
    and Wainwright Evans 115–16
Mitchell, Joe 75
mitral regurgitation 192, 193–5
mitral valve surgery 191–5
MONARC™ device 194

Monitor 261, 262, 263, 265, 266
Morant, Robert 32
Morrison, Herbert 45

Nashef, Samer 198–9, 209–10
    on EuroSCORE 199–208
National Health Service,
    establishment 41–7
National Health Service Act
    (1946) 39, 42, 43, 47
National Network of Pulmonary
    Hypertension clinics 82
Neuberger, James 175
New Scientist, on transplants 135–7
nitric oxide 225
non-beating heart, transfer of
    173–8
normal distribution 203
Norman (domestics man) 241
Norwich 45, 54, 183, 217–18
nurses
    shortage 61
    staffing 272
    views 247–8
Nursing Standard Nurse Awards
    253
nursing standards 247–8

O'Brien, Virginia 253
Olney, Nigel 100, 120
open-heart surgery
    progress in 1970s 101
    steps towards 52–5
operations, numbers, 1958 to
    1964 63
Organ Care System (OCS) 174
organ donation 109–11
Osborne, George 270
O'Sullivan, Michael 194–5

Othello, Staff nurse 241

Paget, James 67
Panorama 110, 135–7
'Papworth Annual' 10–11
Papworth Colony
    expansion 32–3
    Varrier-Jones on work of
        19–30
Papworth Everard village 3, 128,
    238, 253, 274
Papworth Hall 3, 11–13, 32
Papworth Hospital
    in 1990s 257–8
    activity in 2013/14 265
    ambitions 277–8
    buildings 238–9
    facilities 181
    foundation 3
    growth 276
    on itself 237, 248
    mission 267
    move to Addenbrooke's site
        156–7, 257, 258–66, 268–70,
        274–6
    performance above national
        targets 266
    reputation 237
    results 1979 to 1981 102–3
    services 181–219, 237–8, 257–
        8, 271
        see also cardiac surgery;
            cardiology; chest
            medicine; CT scanning;
            measuring outcomes;
            pathology; radiology;
            RSSC; TAVI; TCCA;
            thoracic surgery
    'staff crisis' 137–9

Papworth Hospital (continued)
  staff numbers (2014) 275–6
  as top healthcare employer
    248
  as UK leading centre 181
Papworth Industries 14, 16, 17,
    33–4
Papworth NHS Foundation Trust
    181, 270–4, 276
  culture 273
  leadership 273
  public and staff engagement
    274
  recruitment 274
Papworth Village Settlement
    15–17, 30
Para-aminosalicylic acid 41
Parish, Christopher 47–51, 52–3,
    60, 79, 85
Parker, Rowland, quotes 3–7,
    8–15, 18–19
pathology 188–9
patients
  letters from 239–45
  putting at the heart 245–53
  testimonials 249–53
PDR 228
Peamount 34, 35
Penicillin 48
Pepke-Zaba, Joanna 230
percutaneous transluminal
    angioplasty (PTCA) 183–4
perfusion 55
peripheral vascular surgery 54–5
Petch, Michael 92, 94, 117, 119–
    27, 239
Peterborough 261, 262–4
Pete's club 58
PG-X 224

Philip, Robert 7
pigskin valves 239
Pizzo, Philip 87
Poisson distribution 203
Porter, John 242
Portner, Peer 165
positron emission tomography
    (PET) 187
post-transplant patients 246–7
postoperative death 205–7
Potts Memorial hospital 34
Preston Hall 27, 34, 35
Primary Angioplasty Service 184
printing trade 26–7
private finance initiative (PFI)
    262, 264
Progressive Care Unit 271
prostacyclin 223–4
prostaglandins 223–4
PTCA 183–4
Public Health Laboratory Service
    189
pulmonary embolectomy 226
pulmonary endarterectomy
    (PEA) 216, 229–30
pulmonary hypertension 81–2,
    146, 223–30
  and heart–lung transplantation
    143, 144
pulmonary thromboendarter-
    ectomy (PTE) 225–8

radiology 188–9
  development 79–80
Radner procedure 71
Redfern Inquiry (2008) 81
Reed, Auxiliary nurse 241
rehabilitation 3, 26, 36
Reitz, Bruce 145–6, 147

research and development 267–70, 271–2
Respiratory Support and Sleep Centre (RSSC) 214, 249–50
ring annuloplasty 193
Rintoul, Robert 212
Robertson, Donald 91, 94, 96
Robinson, David 100, 105, 153
Roffey, Hollie 147–8
Rolleston, Humphrey 16
    obituary of Varrier-Jones 30–5
Romberg, Ernst von 223
Roques, François 199–200, 205
Ross, Donald 89
royal visits 13–17
RSSC 214, 249–50
RVADs 233

Salagnac village settlement 34–5
sanatoria 6, 7, 23, 65
SAPIEN™ aortic valve 197
Scadding, Guy 74
Schofield, Peter 194–5
Schroeder, William 162
Scott, John 81
Second World War 42, 48
Seldinger technique 70–1
Sergeant, Paul 206
Sharples, Linda 205, 268
Shipp, Tom 98
Shneerson, John 214
Shumway, Norman 87–8, 93, 127–8, 130–1, 158
Simpson, Horace ('Sam') 244
Skanska 262
skewed distribution 203
sleep disorders 214
Smith, Julian 164–5
smoking 76

Sochocky ('Socky', registrar) 51–2
SOMATOM Force 218–19
Somers, Mr 244
Spiegelhalter, David 81
Stanford University 87–8, 93, 127, 130–1, 147, 158
Stark, John 80, 81
Starzl, Professor 136
Steele, E.H. 241
Stepney, Rob 66–8
Stewart, Susan 81
The Story of Papworth (film) 18
Stott, L.B. 34, 40
Stovin, Peter 80–1
Streptomycin 41
superficial hypothermia technique 53
surgical operations, at Papworth in 1937 39
Surgical Unit 15, 33, 51, 68
survival
    after heart surgery 204, 210–11
    defining 206
SynCardia 168

TAVI 195–7
TCCA 214–16
Thermo Cardiosystems 165
thoracic surgery 217–18
Tracy (patient) 244
Trail, R.R. 39
transcatheter valve implantation (TAVI) 195–7
translational research 267
TransMedics Organ Care System (OCS) 178
Transplant Advisory Panel (TAP) 95, 98–9
Tsui, Steven 161, 168–72, 175

Tubbs, O.S. 40–1
tuberculosis 3–8
  arrest 22–3
  history 3–7
  lung resection for 41
  surgical treatment 65

Ulucan, Huseyin 174–5
Umney, Miss 105
Union internationale contre
    la Tuberculose 35
University of California San
    Diego Medical Centre 228

VADs 232–3
Vane, John 223–4
Vanessa, Nurse ('Auntie Nessie') 241
Varney, Mr 241
Varrier-Jones, Pendrill 8–19
  achievements 30–6
  death 19, 30
  early life 31
  and foundation of Papworth
    3, 8–11
  honours 35
  knighthood 18
  overseas travel 39
  on work of Papworth Colony
    19–30
ventilatory failure 214
ventricular assist devices (VADs)
    232–3
Verney, G.I. ('Bob') 72
village settlements 22–4

Wainwright Evans, David see
    Evans, David Wainwright
waiting-list, at Papworth 133–4
Waksman, Gabriel 41

Wallwork, John
  and animal tissue use 167
  on Bridge 270, 274
  contribution 153–8
  and Flower 80
  on heart 66–8
  on heart–lung transplantation
    143–7, 149, 152, 155–6
  heart–lung transplants
    performed by 147, 150,
    154–5, 245
  and mechanical heart implants
    163, 164
  on Milstein 56–9
  on Papworth move to
    Cambridge 259–60, 270,
    274–6, 277
  published work 81
  and pulmonary hypertension
    treatment 81–2
  and pulmonary thrombo-
    endarterectomy 226
  on vision for future 277
Ward, Donna 248
Wellcome Foundation 224
Wells, Francis 80, 81–2, 115–16,
    192, 193, 218
West Suffolk Hospital 258
Williams, David 120
Wood, Paul 74
Woodhead, German Simms 31,
    32, 240

X-ray Department 68–72

Yacoub, Magdi 127, 145–6
Yellowlees, Henry 95, 96

Zimmern, Ron 257